Principles of Architectural Detailing

PRINCIPLES OF ARCHITECTURAL DETAILING

Stephen Emmitt
Professor of Innovation and Management in Building
Technical University of Denmark

John Olie
Director, Joint Origin, and practising architect,
The Netherlands

Peter Schmid
Emeritus Professor of Architecture and Building
Technology, Eindhoven University of Technology,
The Netherlands

Blackwell
Publishing

Editorial offices:
Blackwell Publishing Ltd, 9600 Garsington Road, Oxford OX4 2DQ, UK
  Tel: +44 (0)1865 776868
Blackwell Publishing Inc., 350 Main Street, Malden, MA 02148-5020, USA
  Tel: +1 781 388 8250
Blackwell Publishing Asia Pty Ltd, 550 Swanston Street, Carlton, Victoria 3053, Australia
  Tel: +61 (0)3 8359 1011

First published 2004 by Blackwell Publishing Ltd

Library of Congress Cataloging-in-Publication Data is available

ISBN 1-4051-0754-5

A catalogue record for this title is available from the British Library

Set in 10½/14 pt Palatino
by Sparks, Oxford – www.sparks.co.uk
Printed and bound in India
by Replika Press Pvt. Ltd, Kundli 131028

The publisher's policy is to use permanent paper from mills that operate a sustainable forestry policy, and which has been manufactured from pulp processed using acid-free and elementary chlorine-free practices. Furthermore, the publisher ensures that the text paper and cover board used have met acceptable environmental accreditation standards.

For further information, visit our website:
www.thatconstructionsite.com

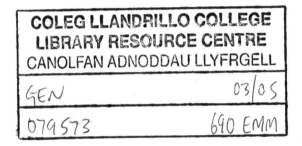

CONTENTS

PREFACE

This is a book about architectural detailing, from the level of the conceptual design through to the physical realisation of design intent during construction. It addresses the creative act of making buildings and introduces concepts and models that we can use to achieve and retain creativity in architecture. It is a product of our collective endeavours as architects and academics striving for a better response to the ecological challenges that we face. Our focus is on the detail – the joint solution – although we have also emphasised the importance of the detail within the overall building design. This is because the act of design is not sequential in the sense of making a conceptual design for the whole building, then the details, then the specification and finally its construction. It is an iterative process in which abstract concepts are developed, tested and redeveloped continually with the aim of producing a set of information from which the building can be constructed. On the one hand the choice of structural systems, services, materials and components is influenced by conceptual design decisions, while on the other hand the conceptual design will be influenced by the details and means of construction. So, when developing conceptual designs for the building we should also be working on conceptual designs for the details. We start with this observation because the conceptual thinking at the level of the detail is vital to the successful construction, maintenance and eventual disassembly of the building and should be included in the early design iterations. This is especially true when using a whole-life approach to our built environment.

There are, to the best of our knowledge, very few books that specifically address the detailing of buildings and the detail design process from first principles. Instead, construction technology books illustrate typical details, providing familiar solutions to common problems, with little explanation as to why they are composed as they are and without much guidance as to the sequence of assembly. Likewise, literature on sustainability tends not to deal with construction details and it is also rather rare for architects to talk about their approach to the materialisation of their designs. As such there is little guidance available to the student of architectural design to help in the development of details from first principles. The result is that both students and practitioners tend to copy the familiar solutions offered in the books, journals and office master files with insufficient thought for the consequences of their actions.

With greater awareness of ecological matters and the environmental impact of buildings on both our health and our planet, we face a challenging future. We can only guess at future climate change and its effects, perceived or otherwise, on our approach to building design, construction, use and reuse. What we do know, however, is that tried and tested approaches to construction may well be inappropriate. It is with this in mind that we have written this book, a modest attempt at encouraging a more ecological approach to architectural detailing from first principles. Our goal was simple – to write a concise book that would help students and practitioners to understand the underlying factors and principles of architectural detailing and the research still required. The contents are deliberately generic so as to appeal to detailers wherever they happen to work, supported by practical examples, checklists and graphics. Likewise, the principles outlined and illustrated are designed to be of equal value to those working with new build, refurbishment and alteration works. Although our book is intended as an introduction to architectural detailing, we have assumed that readers already have a little knowledge of design and construction. To aid clarity we have kept references out of the text; instead we offer some recommended reading in the appendices.

We hope that the book will inform, stimulate, encourage and assist those charged with designing and detailing buildings, leading to an exciting and invigorating environment that respects our health and enriches our planet.

Stephen Emmitt (se@byg.dtu.dk)
John Olie (jointori@euronet.nl)
Peter Schmid (P_Schmid_Prakash@yahoo.com)

Part A
FUNDAMENTAL ISSUES

A1 DETAILING – THE CREATIVE LINK

There is a well-known saying that 'God is in the detail'. Some colleagues report that the famous architect Ludwig Mies van der Rohe first said that 'Gott wohnt im Detail', while others would argue that the quotation is as old as Methuselah. Whatever the truth behind this famous dictum, the point is that the detail is all-important in ensuring high-quality buildings. Indeed, common sense would seem to suggest that the place and meaning of architectural details is paramount, for without the details there would be no building. With increased awareness of environmental issues and the impact of construction activities on our host, the planet, we must consider a more environmentally conscious approach to building design, construction, use, reuse and disassembly. Such a whole-life approach requires a change in our way of thinking, an adjustment to our usual habits, and increased attention to the most challenging of areas – the coming together of materials and processes in a joint solution: the architectural detail. It is here that we face our biggest problems and of course our greatest opportunities for creative thinking and innovation. If we are to adopt a whole-life approach for our built environment, then dealing with joints is unavoidable. Indeed, in order to achieve a cultural architecture in the future it is essential that we deal fundamentally with architectural detail.

Unsettling matters

When designing buildings, architects and engineers tend to be very good at pushing the boundaries of creative endeavour in producing unique and stimulating designs. Styles in architecture and the design approach of architects are constant sources of debate and dialogue in the office and in the media – design

3

sells. Strangely, when it comes to the level of the detail that helps to refine the design concept, the same designers tend to talk differently, if at all, about the thinking behind the detailed design decisions. Perhaps it is just that it is easier to talk in the abstract and conceptual, more interesting to a wider audience than the mechanics of production and realisation. Whatever the reason behind this characteristic we should be concerned that details are not viewed in the same way as the conceptual design – details are undervalued – and this is an unsettling matter given their importance. Unsettling in so much as the time and thinking required to compose and then deliver good quality building is often lacking. It is in the detail, the resolution of joints, that the whole of society is reflected – the way in which we choose and produce building materials, the way we shape components, the way that we execute and assemble buildings, the manner in which we organise labour, the way that we deal with the project economy and the impact of our decisions on our ecology.

So when we start to ask questions such as Why are buildings detailed like they are? and Why do architects and engineers seem to come to the same kinds of solutions every time? it is not easy to find answers. Of course we also need to ask whether we are satisfied with the solutions that are built, and in an age of increased environmental awareness the answer to that last question has to be No. Collectively we need to encourage an innovative approach to detailed design thinking and decision-making, starting with education and taking the principles through into industry. All designers contributing to the built environment need to develop the ability to detail creatively and responsibly with spirit and resolve. For this we need a supportive culture and the time to realise our goals. Fundamentally, we need to loosen up our thinking.

A question of detail

Building design is concerned with solving problems that are specific to a particular client, to a particular site, at a given time. The nature of design is that these problems defy clear definition and therefore require a considerable amount of knowledge to be applied to their resolution. The origin of design problems (often referred to as 'wicked problems') tends to be unclear and the future is always open to question, the outcome of the design process being the creation of a unique design solution, which is then transformed into an equally unique building. The approach taken by individual designers and/or design teams in attempting to resolve the problem before them – the knowledge that they apply – will have a direct influence on the design solution. It follows, therefore, that there is always more than one solution to a problem, regardless of its complexity or perceived familiarity. This is true of large designs and also the design of the component parts and specific joint solution(s).

The interrelationship between conceptual design and construction is paramount to creative detailing (see Fig. A1.1). Decisions made early in the briefing stage will colour and shape the conceptual design, which will influence the subsequent decisions made during the detail design phase. Constraints of production and existing (or available) technologies will also influence this decision-making process that we know as detailing, architectural engineering or materialisation. Limits and opportunities need to be recognised, understood and accommodated; time, finance and resources require careful consideration and evaluation. Furthermore, co-operation, collaboration and co-ordination are essential if design intent is to be realised and transferred effectively to the constructor.

It is very difficult, if not impossible, for one person to possess all of the necessary skills to design, detail and assemble a

Fig. A1.1 People need a more or less tailored built environment that responds to their natural territory and is in harmony with nature.

building. We rely on many individuals and organisations coming together to harness specialist skills and knowledge to the benefit of the project. It is the collective impact of our individual decisions and individual actions (or lack of them) that will impact on the completed artefact, the constructed work. The way that individuals come together and subsequently interact within the structure of the temporary project organisation, the procurement routes used, the time and finance available, and so on will all have an influence on the effectiveness of the detailing and hence affect the performance of the completed building. Since the building will continue in use long after project completion it is vital that the decisions we make are correct. This brings us to another rather fundamental question: Who is in charge of the details? Of all the people and organisations involved with the dynamic yet temporary building project and the building product over its lifetime, do we really know who is responsible for co-ordinating and integrating all of the technological, managerial and design knowledge concerned with the details? Are we really making progress in building and society?

In design offices there is a constant tension between creative design and the detailing phase (see Fig. A1.2). It is here that abstract ideas are converted into specific instructions – encoded in drawings, specifications and schedules – from which the contractor will construct the building. Empathy between conceptual designer and detailer is crucial in ensuring that design intent is adequately represented in the production drawings. This is why, in an ideal world, a conceptual designer should also make conceptual designs for the details, thus helping to ensure continuity between design and production. Failing this, the detailers should have a thorough appreciation and understanding of the conceptual design process, thus helping to maintain and enhance design intent as the design develops. Building design and detailing is not, however, confined to the offices of architects and engineers. Effective detailing requires collaboration with materials suppliers, product manufacturers and specialist trades-people, harnessing their collective knowledge to the benefit of the individual project. Fast-track construction demands effective co-ordination of engineering services, structure and fabric through dedicated information technology networks and effective interpersonal communication. Similarly, the application of lean design and lean construction techniques are

Fig. A1.2 Our built environment in its 'biodiversity' rests on its details.

equally dependent on competent people working in harmony towards a common goal. Design and construction knowledge is best integrated and harnessed through close working relationships, such as alliancing, partnering and the creation of technology clusters, with the ultimate aim of producing a high-quality building that exceeds the client's expectations. The whole should be more than the sum of the part (see Fig. A1.3).

With increased pressure to reduce the time taken to design and construct buildings, combined with associated downward pressure on initial cost and cost-in-use (by far the largest expense), we have seen a decrease in the time dedicated to the detailing process and in many cases a general decline in the quality of thought behind the information produced. With increased complexity of technologies, legislation, environmental concerns and the loss of craft-based knowledge there is a need for more and more information, which takes more time to produce, check and co-ordinate. Although this requirement

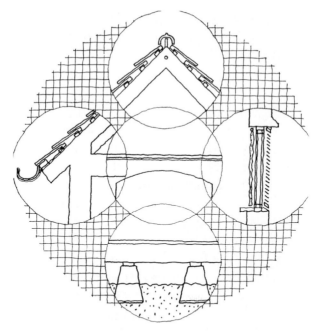

Fig. A1.3   The world of details condensed in a few characteristic ones.

is mitigated by the improvements in information technology, there is still a strong argument for increasing the amount of time dedicated to thinking and reflecting on our detailing and the associated production information. We need time to think about our individual and collective design decisions, adequate time for reflection (and discussion with others) before implementation; indeed, as we argue in this book, we need a suitable philosophical and practical framework in which to make informed decisions.

Creative solutions

If clothes are our second skins, then surely buildings are our third. We spend the majority of our time in and around buildings, be it at work, rest or play. Just as the wrong choice of clothes can make us uncomfortable, so too can the materials that we choose for our buildings and the way in which they are put together. Conversely, when we get the choice right we feel comfortable and confident and experience a sense of wellbeing. Conceptual and detail design decisions relating to material selection and their juxtaposition will affect the manner in which we perceive and interact with our built environment and will directly influence our physical and mental health, hopefully in a positive manner.

In spite of our rather obvious observations about the fundamental importance of the architectural detail, we are repeatedly confronted with problems during the construction process and with the finished building, regardless of the type of procurement route adopted and the inherent level of complexity. Many of these problems are a direct consequence of careless or inappropriate detailing during the design phase or careless implementation during construction. Once spotted, these difficulties often seem insurmountable, thus leading some to claim, somewhat cynically, that it is 'the Devil who is in the detail'. With the benefit of hindsight we often find that it is the quality of thought behind the detail, both in design and execution, which is lacking. In essence these would appear to be problems brought about by a failure to apply our knowledge and skills in an appropriate way. In our search for creative solutions that work, we first need to give some thought to the underlying reasons behind the apparent lack of attention to detailing in practice. We need to look at the construction sector and to the education of design and construction professionals.

The construction sector

As construction technologies have evolved and buildings have become more complex in both design and assembly we have witnessed the development of specialists and the fragmentation of the building 'team'. Manufacturing, both on and off site, the increased importance of specialist suppliers and subcontractors, diversification of professionals, the tendency to outsource and sub-subcontract work, concerns over risk avoidance and confusion over responsibility for different elements of the work all contribute to an interesting and dynamic working environment; however, we are often left to ponder who is really in charge of design quality. When the outcome is good we all like to claim credit, but when there are problems it seems impossible to find anyone willing to own up to their responsibilities. The diverse and often competing organisations that contribute to the temporary construction project must interact, that is, they also must come together as a temporary joint solution, at various stages through the life of a project. With increased diversification has come greater complexity of the organisational joints (if we may use such a term) and with it a more pressing need to really understand the interface between professionals, a concern that can sometimes overshadow the interrelationship of materials.

It is often difficult to find evidence of long-term thinking in the construction sector because of the focus on short-term project objectives. Attention tends to be on lower initial cost and ever-faster completion times, working with outdated economic models and project management tools that fail to adequately address quality and environmental concerns. Indeed, with some notable exceptions, we have yet to embrace a whole-life approach to the construction and use of buildings. Clients, their professional advisers and politicians all share a responsibility here; we could and should do more.

Built environment education programmes

Over the past 20 or so years there has been a gradual shift in the content of architectural programmes towards creativity at the expense of technology. Likewise, many of the construction-related courses have moved towards management skills at the expense of technology. Obviously, it is possible to put only so much content into a particular programme of study, but the result of this shift is that we have architects who are not adequately educated in the benefits of construction technology and managers who do not fully appreciate the technology and processes that they are charged with managing. We have also witnessed site operatives who, when faced with something slightly unfamiliar, are completely lost as to how to solve the problem, simply because they do not understand the underlying principles inherent in how buildings go together, reflecting a decline in skills training. This fundamental inability to teach some basic principles (and transferable skills) has resulted in us becoming over-reliant on copying and trusting the judgement of others; that is, we have lost the ability to question why things are how they are. In many cases the result is, at best, mediocre detailing; at worst there are difficulties with constructability, latent defects, ensuing maintenance problems and further down the line associated problems with disassembly, which someone has to rectify and pay for. From our current perspective it appears that we have lost the art of creative detailing (see Fig. A1.4).

The current approach in architectural education is to emphasise the 'great' gesture and creative design proposals – architecture with a capital 'A'. Such emphasis is often at the expense of the equally creative and vital issue of the technologies and the managerial skills required to first assemble the building and then to operate it. Small, apparently, is not beautiful. A useful comparison can be made with science. While nuclear physics became a key for a better understanding of matter as well as an

(a)

(b)

(c)

Fig. A1.4   (a–c) Detailing was, is and remains a precondition for each building in the past, in the present and in the future.

important knowledge base for numerous other disciplines, 'nuclear' architecture (if we may make this comparison) has yet to be discovered. Arguably, we remain overly concerned with the bigger picture and not with the pixels that compose it. Taking our cue from science, we argue that this missing link has urgently to be transformed into a creative link. Quality buildings demand quality thought, quality detailing and quality assembly. In some respects this missing link is starting to take shape in the form of the architectural engineering and architectural technology disciplines where the design of the details and the importance of engineering as a creative discipline are given far more prominence than is currently the case in architectural education. These new programmes are an interesting development that will, eventually, have a positive effect on the way in which we detail buildings. We do, however, still have a way to go.

Looking back at the recorded history of our built environment to the highlights of architecture and building technology, we can identify and recognise the knowledge and control exerted over the connection of materials, building parts, components and elements that made the masterpieces possible (see Fig. A1.5). Such buildings demonstrate a commitment to design vision, excellence in detailing and engineering solutions and of course great tenacity and determination to see the project through. Of course the less well-detailed and poorly crafted buildings were quick to collapse or to be replaced, thus even here our focus is directed to that which has been successful and which is deemed important by society. Drawing from the information embedded in the buildings around us we can see how our own ideas are confirmed. Details – connections, joints and knots – have an extraordinarily crucial place and meaning, both technologically and culturally. Nevertheless we often fail to provide the necessary attention to the details in our daily practice, distracted by other, seemingly more important issues.

This is a criticism that can also be aimed at education and research. Lack of a proper devotion to the details causes difficulties not only for designers and contractors (the experts) but also for the building users (the layperson) because it is the users who interact with the building on a daily basis over a period of many years. However, we must not be too negative. While bearing in mind that ineffective detailing is undesirable, in this book we want to emphasise the potential that effective detailing

(a)

(b)

Fig. A1.5   (a,b) Different times, different materials, different approaches, clearly recognisable in the detail.

has to offer. In particular we would like to support the experts and students (the future experts) in the field of architectural design and assist in their commitment to creative detailing. Designers and engineers should have a greater say and hence more impact on the manner in which the conceptual design is realised. In the majority of cases it is not sufficient or acceptable to delegate this task to others who may not necessarily share the same values and goals. To do so requires a greater understanding of the subject.

The place and meaning of architectural details

Details are determined by their place of origin and their meaning. Science, art, technology and wisdom are the components that need to be brought together in the design and production of details. Design and technology can be dealt with through good education, comprehensive briefing and the professional management of design intent from inception to completion and beyond. Underlying this is a fundamental requirement for synthesis and integration towards an ecological approach.

Place

The place of architectural details can be 'located' on quite different levels. Some of the most significant of these, which are interconnected, are discussed briefly here.

- Architectural details have their place within each and every building structure. It is the sum of those details that collectively determines the structure and fabric of a building. They combine to form space and enclosure, and between them there are 'only' connecting lines or materials arranged according to the instructions given in the production information.
- Architectural details are the preconditions of any building structure. Their 'strategic' place collectively determines the main shape or form of a building structure. But at the same time – looking carefully – they also determine the *gestalt* of a building. Properly detailed means precisely designed, even in the smallest dimensions.
- Architectural details are parts of a phenomenon; their place can be found everywhere and in everything, in the sense that they are the connections, joints and knots which keep the whole of an object and building in its place.

Meaning

The meaning of architectural details can be found in a variety of guises, depending on our point of view.

■ Architectural details express, mainly visually, a certain concept and design approach. As characteristic parts of a whole building they can carry a typical signature, a specific language, and communicate messages to users, society and of course architectural critics.

■ Architectural details reflect the cultural background from which they come and in which they are 'born'. Often they breathe the atmosphere and show the 'colour' of their cultural context.

■ Architectural details, according to their scale (and place), represent a kind of 'cosmos', which is one of the main determinants of each and every building, moving from the micro to the macro and vice versa.

The place and meaning of architectural details can be understood as a certain whole. On the one hand it can be seen that the detail is an extraordinarily important part, which exerts its entire impact on the whole. On the other hand there is the ancient concept of 'as in the large, in the small', in that the whole also exerts itself on the parts. It follows that we can imagine the whole (building) and its details as being the 'same'. Indeed, both are normally the result of the same manufacturing and design style.

Technique and technology both have their etymological roots in the old Greek term *techne*, which means the art to make an artefact (Fig. A1.6), to materialise, to build. From our

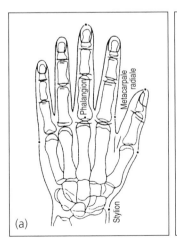
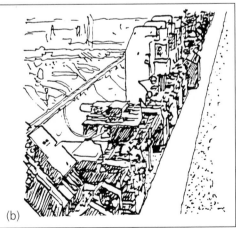

(a)   (b)

Fig. A1.6 (a,b) Two worlds of production, one with flowing transitions, one with sharp limits, and always with its own character.

current viewpoint we see two main approaches to the production of buildings and their details (although we should recognise that this is not possible everywhere in the world). These may be either, or a combination of, hand-made or machine-made.

Presently we are experiencing an enormous amount of technological development, a race towards complete automation (Fig. A1.7), supported by computer-aided design (CAD) and computer-aided manufacturing (CAM), and recently a strong tendency for virtual reality approaches and applications. Our attention to the machine-made is often at the expense of the hand-made which, of course, is still valid. Indeed, a huge part of the world population relies on hand-made approaches and human labour, a rather large proportion of which is in urgent need of a 'roof' and a supply of clean water. The hand-made procedures, therefore, are at least as important as the machine-made ones in our small world. We not only need virtual buildings but desperately seek the means to provide *real* buildings.

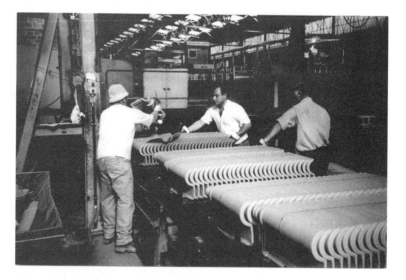

Fig. A1.7 Highly automated roof tile factory (Portugal). Quality control was undertaken best by experienced workers, following problems with mechanised systems.

Supporting an ecological approach

These observations bring us to the subject of ecological sustainability, which is strongly related to inequality in the world. This means that we have to save our resources, especially energy, and make a greater effort to use materials and space much better than we do at present. We have to avoid deterioration, exploitation and pollution as side effects of manufacturing, producing, using and recycling buildings. The argument for designing buildings that are environmentally friendly over their entire lifetime is well established, but the philosophy has been slow to find its way into normal practice. The concept of a building as a generator of waste, in its conception, during its long life and in its death (and possible rebirth), is an important one. Too often we are concerned only with the completion of a project, forgetting that it is during its use that a building, aided and abetted by its inhabitants, is particularly wasteful of energy and resources.

Decisions made early in the design process and the manner in which the structure, fabric and services are detailed and subsequently assembled will greatly influence the energy efficiency of the building. These detail decisions will also influence the ease with which the building can be adapted over its lifetime to accommodate changing user needs, and the ease, or otherwise, of disassembly and recycling or disposal of redundant materials. We must, therefore, focus on a harmonious and ecological approach to construction, use and reuse of our buildings and their constituent parts.

The dominating mechanical connections that tend to characterise architectural details are not necessarily the only ones available and applicable in building technology. Within this book we would also like to explore the possibilities of joining and connecting things, materials and components through familiar and rarely used techniques. First, and at the most fundamental level, we must recognise the force or power of attraction, which is the basis of adhesion, cohesion and gravitation. There are manifestations of this force on different scales and in various fields. Certain typical details, knots, joints and connections are to be found in:

- atoms, molecules and cells
- mechanical, chemical and magnetic circumstances
- solar, galactic and external galactic systems.

Nature provides us with some extraordinarily sustainable characteristics (see Fig. A1.8). In nature there is very little waste and the concept of 'durability' is interpreted differently to the building sector. It might be useful, therefore, to study our natural environment more than we have done in our recent past, with the aim of joining 'biotics' with 'eco design' in order

Fig. A1.8 Sustainable nature. Sustainable concepts and models manifested in micro-, meso- and macro-cosmos.

to develop innovative concepts for detailed design solutions. It may be self-evident as to what we need for an ecologically robust building technology and the details that belong to it. Nevertheless, there are a few substantial rules to be found in nature that can be applied to detailing, especially those of minimising and maximising. We need to minimise our use of materials, energy, deterioration, exploitation, pollution and sick building syndrome. For example, 'zero energy' houses that are also healthy to live in are a realistic possibility. Sustainable materials and renewable energy sources should be promoted. We also need to maximise the higher qualities, namely, humane working conditions, health and comfort, flexibility, multifunctionality, decentralised (regional) production, reuse, recycling, biodegradability and quality of life (see Fig. A1.9).

Details, although mostly small, are complex objects. Therefore, it is necessary to combine knowledge and experience from diverse disciplines and integrate them in the detail. Hence, the detail becomes an embodiment of our collective knowledge. For

Fig. A1.9 Individual, social, technical and environmental issues. They all play an important role in building and detailing.

a responsible and sustainable choice of building materials there is a simple tool that has been developed with knowledge about the possible origins and treatments of building materials – the basic model of architectural detailing (see Chapter A4 and Section B). We can guess (with relative ease) what impact the materials have had in the past, are having at present and are likely to have in the future on both the environment and our health, and such issues can be addressed through the basic model. From this we are able to progress to typical joint solutions (see Fig. A1.10) and their subsequent analysis and refinement for a more sustainable solution (see Section C). To detail the joints and ensure their correct application on the construction site requires a combination of effective management and collaboration – a systematic approach to designing and developing details based on teamwork.

Beside a systematic approach to construction it is extremely important that we urgently strive for a certain quality. The quality that we are referring to is concerned with our health and our environment in a holistic sense. It may, unfortunately, never be possible to reach the highest level of quality in any real sense, but attempts should be made to at least consider a principle of wholeness in the life cycle of buildings and its components. It is, however, not possible to give a precise recipe that describes how to reach the desired qualities, other than to set out the required quantities through performance and functional requirements.

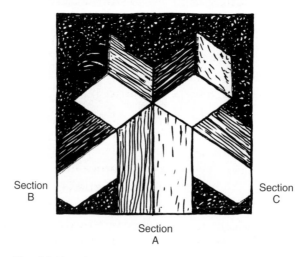

Section
B

Section
C

Section
A

Fig. A1.10   Directions in detailing – three, joining in one connection, like Sections A, B and C of this book (a Japanese knot).

Instead, an awareness of the values and principles, in addition to regulations and systems, can go some way in helping to achieve these higher qualities of life. We must be able and willing to champion the product through the application of innovative solutions that are ecologically sound and offer value to all stakeholders.

Agenda

Short- and long-term thinking both belong to a holistic view of the entire life cycle of the constructed works. This is an essential condition for the effective handling of the conceptual and the detailed design, and will go a long way towards a responsible and sustainable approach to construction, building use and recycling. All three authors of this book have tried, in their own way, to work towards a practical yet philosophically sound approach to architectural detailing. Our work has been explored in the daily task of practising architecture and also in the more rarefied academic world, essentially the fusion of theory and practice. In the chapters that follow we will draw on our collective experience to advance a practical and scientific foundation for architectural detailing.

The argument presented here starts with some fundamental issues in Section A. If we are to rediscover the art of detailing then we need to start by addressing two interrelated questions. First, do we need a philosophy of detailing? Second, how do details develop? Once these have been addressed we are then better informed to look at a model to assist with the detail design decision-making process, the basic model of architectural detailing. This comprehensive nine-cell matrix, with the detail (the knot) at its centre, is a decision-making tool that encourages architectural detailing from an environmentally aware perspective and forms the heart of the book. The model has been developed, tested in practice and refined with the sole aim of helping the designer to make decisions.

Section B has nine chapters, each one representing a cell in the basic model. Each chapter provides philosophical and practical information to assist the detailer with his or her design decision-making process. The cells are designed to stimulate thinking and help designers to generate ideas and information, and a limited number of keywords are offered to help in this regard. The detailer is then able to analyse, (re)design and apply creative, yet practical, joint solutions that we hope are more environmentally friendly than the standard solutions.

Once we are familiar with the underlying issues and have a robust framework to assist our decision-making then we are able to look at the development of architectural details from first, environmentally sound, principles. Section C provides practical guidance on the development of details and the management of the detailing process. We develop a typology of joints, develop our vocabulary of details and then propose a nine-plus-one step model that enables the detailer to develop more sustainable solutions for particular joints. We conclude by looking at the managerial challenge inherent in developing and implementing creative architectural details and consider the benefits of collaborative working. Collectively we need to think differently and hence do things differently, that is, innovate in both the process and the product, take a more considered view and champion the sustainable product.

A2 THE PHILOSOPHY OF DETAILING

Given the importance of the detailing process and its impact on all our lives, we need to raise a number of fundamental issues. Do we need something like a philosophy of detailing? Is detailing not a simple task which has to be solved technologically, practically and economically – the process of making? Or is detailing, assuming that the designer has already some love for it, just a matter of styling? The answers to these questions are to be found in the simple observation that design is about making choices, and this applies at all levels of design. To make decisions we cannot do without the guiding mechanism of style rules, which help us with the 'why' and the 'how' questions. An answer to the question of 'why' calls for a philosophy, an attitude towards the world around us. An answer to the question of 'how' calls for hard and practical morphological solution principles. This means that the style rules themselves must be as operational and practical as possible. Having a wonderful philosophy is essential to get started, but is not sufficient to get things done.

A philosophy

In human culture we observe paradigms, formulations and definitions in nearly all fields, sectors or disciplines. Sometimes these are quite explicit, sometimes more subtle and implied, yet there is hardly an important (political or commercial) decision made without some form of scientific exploration and explanation underpinning that decision. Although we know that sciences can also be misused, it is necessary to ground designs as well as processes of realisation on clear and fundamental theories. Hence Kurt Lewin's well known dictum: 'There's nothing so practical as a good theory.' But looking at the scientific base of architecture, building technology and detailing, we hardly find anything that could answer the quest for an intellectual and philosophical embedding of the daily process of detailing in architecture and building technology. This is an extraordinary observation given that we have been building and writing about building for a long time.

There is an established body of literature that addresses how we design, both as generic designers and more specifically as designers of buildings. This knowledge base continues to grow, but with very little investigation into the detailed area of architectural design where the design concepts are materialised. Few authors have attempted to philosophise about detail design decision-making, preferring to stick with conceptual design, which they regard as a much more creative process than the events that turn the concepts into real buildings. We also see a definite division between the literature on architecture and that concerned with the construction process, with a very small amount of literature dedicated to architectural design management. Compare this, for example, with the field of new product development, which offers a more integrated approach between design, production and the management of the process, both in the literature and in practice. While this body of literature is particularly relevant to the development of new building products, it also provides a number of pointers to a more integrated and knowledge-based approach (see Fig. A2.1) to architectural design and construction, an argument developed here.

Continuing with the theme of integration and the knowledge-based approach to problem-solving, we can put forward a number of hypotheses (see Fig. A2.2) with the aim of devel-

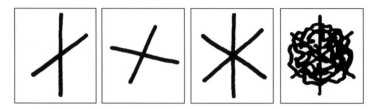

Fig. A2.1 Building a philosophy – getting a grip on complexity. Even the most complex and complicated structure 'starts' with the simple intent of joining one part to another.

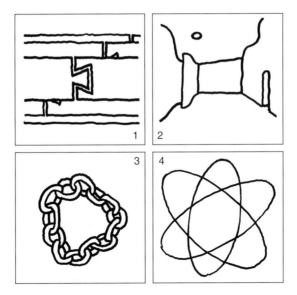

Fig. A2.2 The four hypotheses: (1) Combine, connect, join similar, various or different parts, materials or components. (2) Integrate diverse elements towards equilibrium (sometimes dynamic). (3) Bring parts together (that is what building means) for a certain (predetermined) period of time. (4) The 'knot' is the 'nucleus' of a building and of building system(s). All are in order to construct a new whole – a whole building, to create a harmonious, well-balanced artefact.

oping a philosophy of architectural detailing. There are three fundamental hypotheses to consider.

- *Hypothesis 1:* The art and technology to build is based on the skill to combine, to connect and to join similar, various or different parts, materials or components in order to construct a new whole: a building.
- *Hypothesis 2:* Architecture is the combination and integration of diverse elements to create a harmonious and well-balanced artefact, by which its elements are the boundaries that create spaces.
- *Hypothesis 3:* To build means simply to bring parts together and then sustain the whole for a certain (predetermined) period of time.

Taking our cue from our natural world we find evidence supporting all three hypotheses all around us. If we look at how matter in nature is 'constructed' we see that time and time again there are 'small parts' arranged and structured in such a way that they form a 'larger part'. Using various forms and dimensions of attraction and attachment the whole cosmos appears as a structure or architecture based on the *gestaltung* and composition of smaller particles. This would appear to be valid from the microcosm to the macrocosm. So in architecture we can speak of a nucleus and atoms, which determine the quality of the (next) bigger structure.

The elementary yet essential phenomenon of connection can also be observed in many different guises. For example, different combinations of chemicals result in a multitude of quite different substances and are exploited by chemists to produce a multitude of different products for the worldwide marketplace. Literature and poetics combine words to create art; indeed the structure of our language can even be used as a cue to develop a 'language of detail', as we will see in a later chapter. Similarly we experience music because of the composition of sounds and rhythms. Human society is obviously dependent on how people of many different backgrounds and cultures interact. Mostly this connection is harmonious and enjoyable, although failure to make the right connections can lead to stress and conflict. The term religion, from the Latin *re-ligare*, to bind again, shows, independent of any specific belief, denomination, faith or confession, the archetypal reason for human beings to be more or less connected or bound with the essence of life. For example, in Japan we find many rituals in which binding, connecting, joining and knotting play an important role in everyday life, a characteristic also to be found in other cultures. Symbolically as well as practically, in the sense that ritual buildings are often bound, e.g. from grass, we can see and experience how elementary the connection or knot is to life. Whatever word we choose to use – binding, combining, connecting, joining, knotting or even uniting – in architecture nothing can happen, stay in place or retain its shape without the act of bringing parts together, joining them together and keeping them together for a certain period of time.

Konrad Wachsmann was one of the forerunners in understanding the detail, or the knot, as reported in his 1959 publication *Wendepunkt im Bauen* (published in English in 1961 as *The Turning Point of Building*). Wachsmann called for attention to the detail in a fundamental way and urged designers to respond to the technologies of the (machine) age. It is an inspirational book that helped to draw our attention to details and their fundamental importance in architecture and construction. It is not only the functional and spatial composition that makes the building possible and characteristic, but also the detailed way in which the materials and components are brought together and held together in a particular place.

As argued above, the success of a built structure is, to a very large extent, dependent on the quality of the details, which have been neglected in the last few decades. Design education, therefore, should have a (re)new(ed) focus on how to really make buildings, particularly building systems, and how to connect the parts (in the details). We need to rediscover the lost art of detailing and respond to the environmentally friendly technologies of our age. Now (once again) we need concepts for building systems including their detailing. This brings us to our fourth hypothesis. The knot is the concrete base of each building system, of each building method and finally of each building.

- *Hypothesis 4:* The knot is the *nucleus* of a building and of the building system(s).

From a philosophical and practical stance we can see that where materials or building components meet each other – at the points, at the lines or at the planes or surfaces – there is nothing. This 'nothingness' may be very narrow or very small, however this border zone is a kind of 'essence' around which physical material is arranged. We are, of course, referring to the all-important joint – the joint solution – that lies at the heart of our details.

As already implied our human inventions are often inspired by, or even copied from, models to be found in nature (see Fig. A2.3). In the frame of a philosophical exploration of detailing it is essential to be aware of details to be found in nature, obvious examples being the beauty and strength of the spider's web (the silk is comparatively much stronger than anything man-made), the cellular structure of plants and the beauty of seashells. Such details are manifest in the whole macro- and micro-cosmos, but most near at hand in the meso-cosmos, which we experience and perceive directly via our sense organs. In parallel with our rather mechanistic approach to design and construction it may be rewarding to also study natural

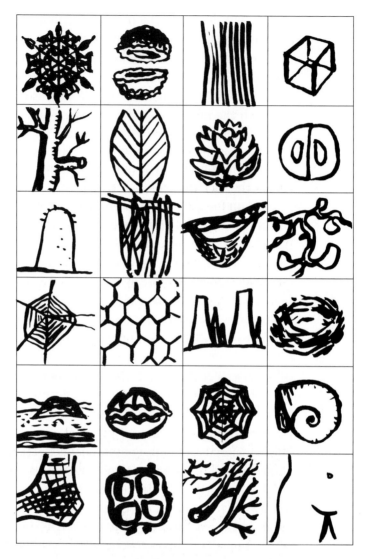

Fig. A2.3 Examples from nature: all connections, joints, knots based on structures in nature. Inspiring examples, models, concepts (systematically studied in bionics and/or ecodesign).

structures – their composition, construction and details – along with their process of growth, decay and rebirth.

The scientific field of bionics is concerned with the study of natural processes and natural objects. Here we find the most interesting, surprising and beautiful phenomena. We also find concepts, examples and models for man-made objects, artefacts and art. Architectural bionics, sometimes called ecological design, has a lot of potential. Efficient and beautiful inspirations about how to build, what to build and which 'architecture' could be designed are some of the possibilities. The recognised efficiency in this is mainly based on a kind of natural drive to minimise material usage for a certain purpose. The 'minimum principle' is one of the most influential forces in the construction of natural structures and a philosophy reflected in minimal engineering strategies, and to a certain extent 'lean' production and management techniques.

In a philosophical background for building we have to address the fact that construction activities have a substantial impact on the quality of our environments and hence our quality of life (Fig. A2.4). Since we face a worldwide environmental catastrophe in terms of exploitation, pollution and deterioration because of overconsumption, where building activities are responsible for approximately one-third of all consumed resources and energy, we have to take much more care to conserve and enhance our resources wherever possible. Furthermore, we are confronted with sick building syndrome (SBS), for which design and construction practices are fully responsible. This is a disease of our own making and one that could be eradicated with a little more thought in the design phase for the impact of the materials selected and their effect on our health and wellbeing.

Fig. A2.4 Roof detailing. The flat roof needs expensive and disruptive reparation every ten years or so and is a well-known source of problems in wet climates. By comparison the pitched roof needs less maintenance with an average of 50 years between reparations. The pitched roof is a better example of detailing with nature than the flat roof.

Environmental issues and sick building syndrome are both becoming more prominent areas for research and consultancy, responding to the problems we face. Surely, this must force us to consider them not only as something to look for but also as cultural and social challenges. In this sense we should be able to provide an answer to these problems from the core skills inherent in designing and conceptualising buildings, that is, through their knots. The logical conclusion is to undertake an environmental impact assessment (EIA) as well as a health impact assessment (HIA) at critical stages during the design and construction process (see Fig. A2.5). These assessment tools belong to the very preliminary acts in the design process, including the design of the details and associated selection of the materials.

As stated earlier, the knot is the essential condition and a kind of driving force behind the whole of a structure of a system or a building. Hence the knot determines the physical and readily perceived qualities of the building, while also determining the higher qualities concerning our health and wellbeing within

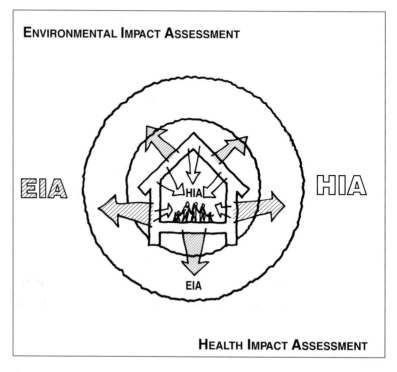

Fig. A2.5 Health impact assessment (HIA) and environmental impact assessment (EIA): both a must for responsible decision-making.

our immediate environs. In principle the knot is theoretically embedded now: the phenomenon of the knot is recognised as a part of a given natural context. At the same time it is anchored within various systems, reflecting its principle, which is valid in all grown and built structures. Moreover in its quality it is like a nucleus within the core of an atom, the essential co-creating force and key for the structure of the next bigger whole(s) – the knot as a metaphor (see Chapter A4).

Making choices

Now that we have our hypothesis we can look at design and the decision-making processes that help to realise our design intent. The point has already been made about the lack of investigation into architectural detailing. One reason for this is the (wrongly held) belief that detailing is a relatively clear-cut activity, best carried out by individuals with technical rather than design skills. To the uninitiated this may be the impression given, particularly as the main materials and construction systems are determined during the development of the conceptual design. Moving from the conceptual to the detail design is akin to moving from the undefined to the defined, from the infinite to the finite, an iterative decision-making process aimed at narrowing down the options to a solution, an appropriate answer, to the problem. So we could conclude that the design and detailing phases need different skills, the first creative and the second pragmatic, with the detailing merely a means to an end. To a certain extent this is true, but both the conceptual and detail phases need the input of both creative and pragmatic skills to realise the design intent and hence provide value for the client. It follows that it is crucial to assemble the right people for the right task, that is, professionals with complementary competences who are committed to quality and who are able to co-operate and share knowledge to the benefit of all actors. Creative work on the details should be fed back into the conceptual ideals of the overall design proposal as part of ongoing iterations, thus the design (and even the client's initial requirements) develops and evolves as knowledge is introduced and synthesised.

Architectural detailing is clearly considerably more than a task-based decision-making activity. It is a knowledge-centred activity that bristles with equal creative endeavour as the larger conceptual design phase and of course is linked to the conceptual development of the details themselves. In the majority of the literature on design decision-making the process is described as an information-processing activity, which to a certain extent it is, but this is not the entire picture. Rather it is about communication, building and sharing knowledge, collaboration and making collective decisions. Design is a knowledge-based decision-making process that results in a set of information from which the building may be constructed, used and maintained. As designers and detailers we need to make decisions every day, this is what our profession is: indeed, that is what we are paid for. Our decisions must be made within an economic, legislative and ethical framework in which we have to consider the element of risk associated with each and every decision. This is rarely an easy task because we are dealing with 'wicked' problems and creative processes in which it is unusual to have all the information available to us that is required to make a rational decision. Therefore we have to apply our professional judgement. On a fundamental level our decisions are coloured by three interrelated areas: (1) the organisational culture of the design/engineering office, (2) the project culture, and (3) the characteristics of the individual decision-maker (especially our knowledge-processing ability). The intention is to develop a dynamic relationship between whole-life cost, quality, value and the attendant risks associated with possibilities and preferences (see Fig. A2.6).

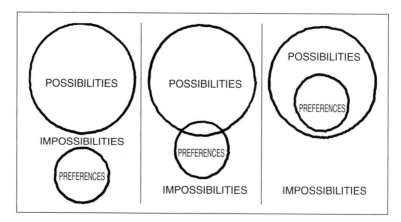

Fig. A2.6 (Limited) possibilities and (wishful) preferences – wherever they may occur – are seldom far from each other and also seldom identical with each other, but fortunately they may overlap.

Possibilities and preferences

Design starts with an inventory of criteria and constraints (the initial client brief). This helps to determine the 'solution space' in which we search for and develop possibilities, ideas and concepts for a design and its details. This is what is expected of designers – developing and presenting a collection of variants that comply with and enhance the client brief, adding value to an expressed need. For example, presenting three different options to a client allows the client and those associated with the design to discuss, think, compare and 'weigh' each concept; only then can we start to get to the real preferences and hence realistic possibilities. But these values must be based on common values that we all strive for – common ownership of the design and its associated values, participation and inclusivity. We must constantly strive to make the best choices from the possibilities available to us. We must address the preferences and the values of our client and of society as a whole.

Using knowledge in new ways

We may benefit from looking at areas of knowledge that lie outside the field of construction. We have already made the point about looking at biology as a source of ideas from which to stimulate innovation, and there are other areas. For example, the field of new product design offers a variety of tools and models that integrate design and production through innovation and collaboration. Other industries that design and build unique products, for example shipbuilding, provide other routes to explore for inspiration and technological transfer. Whatever our source of inspiration we should recognise that the principles of detailing are most commonly based on shared experience.

Mechanisms to promote long-term thinking

In building it is common to rely on our experience, in other words to look to our past. By doing so we can learn a lot about the behaviour of buildings in use and hence make some qualified assumptions about the future, especially if we concentrate on the applied principles of building. The constructed work has a lifetime in which to perform a positive (or negative) function for the users in terms of functionality, health and environment (see Fig. A2.7). It is important to extend lifetime thinking and make a real link between the maintenance of the building and the management of the facility. We may come up with a nice design, but what does it mean in the longer term? What is the impact on the users' health and wellbeing? The building design and proposed method of construction should also include its lifetime prognosis – from execution, its desired durability, its maintenance, its renovation potential, its functionality as user patterns change, its recycling potential, its potential 'biography'.

Time to start again?

Solutions to problems tend to be gradual and based on what went before. In many cases we are adding new parts to details to meet new (improved) performance requirements and changes in regulations. This may be acceptable up to a certain point, but the danger in the majority of cases is that the detail starts

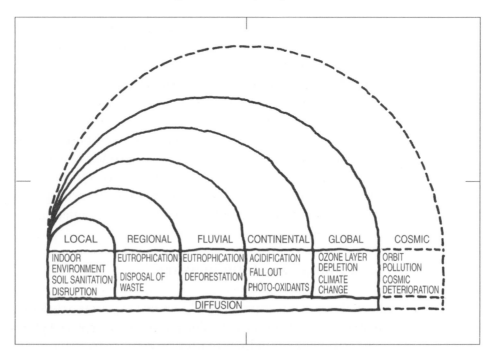

Fig. A2.7   Impact on the environment by building. Adapted and extended from the five-level model of the Dutch Environmental Policy Plan, 1989.

to become overcomplicated. This can cause difficulties with constructability and invariably leads to wasted materials and cost. Instead, it may be beneficial to take a fresh look at why the detail is as it is and start again, and learn to constantly question our habits and be open to new ideas and concepts. For example, a change in building codes or regulations may be an excellent incentive for trying a fresh approach rather than adjusting what worked previously. To do so, however, requires the two precious commodities of time and resources, both of which are in short supply. So the question of whether a fresh look at our details should be carried out within a project context (that is, paid for by the client) or whether it should be undertaken as part of the design organisation's ongoing development (that is, paid for out of overheads) may be a difficult one to deal with. What is certain is that members of the design office and collaborating partners must be given adequate time to undertake the task thoroughly.

There are two approaches. The first is to deconstruct the familiar detail, break it down into the base elements, investigate and analyse why the parts are as they are and try to rebuild the detail so that it is simpler. There are examples from practice where architects, engineers, manufacturers and constructors meet as a technology cluster to do just this. Their aim is to improve the detail in terms of performance, constructability and value through the sharing of knowledge. Various techniques may be used within this environment to generate creative solutions, ranging from the familiar brainstorming technique first proposed by Alex Osborn in 1953 through to more process-based models of problem-solving based on checklists. The problem with this approach is that our thinking is coloured by the very detail that we are looking at, hence 'new' solutions are primarily incremental improvements, an observation which also applies to 'case based' reasoning. We need to get back to first principles.

The second approach is to start entirely from first principles and ignore the standard solution. Again a team is assembled and charged with addressing the problem, although the difference here is that no information about the detail is allowed (most of us will, however, still be preconditioned by our previous experiences). One question will suffice: What are we trying to achieve? Although this may sound a little extreme it can be effective in generating creative ideas which later can be worked up into practical details. Brainstorming may still be used: however, it is a little easier in this context to push the boundaries by engaging in synetics as developed by William Gordon, drawing analogies between elements of the problem and similar problems in very different fields. Synetics is based on making the familiar strange and the strange familiar. An example would be of the snake shedding its skin as it grows: Is this analogous to changing the building fabric as the building use changes? We are looking for a leap in knowledge.

Both approaches may be valid; indeed it may be beneficial to approach the problem from both directions in an attempt to find common ground.

A3 DEVELOPING DETAILS

We have identified the need for a philosophical understanding and underpinning of detailing and have also highlighted the importance of our decisions. Before we turn to the more practical guidance of the basic model of architectural detailing it is necessary to understand where details come from and how they are developed. Earlier we identified our concern about the lost art of detailing. Here we take a closer look at the underlying factors essential for learning this art from first principles. What information do we need? In an information-rich world, where do we start?

A suitable starting point

There is a well-worn joke that goes something like this. A stranger to a region stops a passer-by and asks for directions to a nearby town. The passer-by pauses for a second and replies 'I wouldn't start from here.' Over the years some of our students (strangers to detailing) have received similar replies when asking us (the studio instructor) how to detail their building design. The construction technology books provide illustrations of standard solutions to relatively familiar detailing problems and are a valuable source of reference. This type of book shows the detail as it will appear when assembled, but does not explain the decision-making process that goes before, nor for that matter the sequence of assembly. So the stranger to the subject of detailing is not given advice on how to get to a particular solution. Not surprisingly the tendency is to copy the detail from the textbook without necessarily understanding how and why it is composed as it is or how it is to be assembled on site (Fig. A3.1). This makes it very difficult to start from first principles when confronted by an unfamiliar detailing problem. It also makes it

Fig. A3.1   Joint solution (Slovenia). A kind of dense wickerwork of timber dovetail connections, forming a strong wall around a water well.

very difficult to question (critically evaluate) the familiar solution. The starting point, therefore, is very important.

As students we come to our chosen subject with enthusiasm and energy, and not without a degree of trepidation. We rely on our lecturers for guidance, or at least advice on a sensible starting point. This all-important starting point will be coloured, dare we say determined, by the course of study chosen. For example, architects (the designers) begin with the big idea and start to focus in on the detail as the design develops, essentially a deductive approach to design. Architectural technologists and architectural engineers (the detailers) are more likely to begin with the details and work outwards towards the conceptual design, an inductive approach to design. These starting points are a direct result of different educational programmes and reflect interests in particular areas of building design. We must, therefore, recognise that these distinct professional groups are likely to approach detailing differently. As such they are ideally suited to working together on the same project. Each will be trying to solve a particular issue to the best of their ability, with the available resources and in the available time. Ideally a balanced professional will adopt both deductive and inductive strategies simultaneously. By working in harmony the creative architect and the pragmatic technologist/engineer will develop a constructive and creative link: our starting point.

Detailing joints

The majority of details have evolved over time in response to local building traditions, innovative technologies and legislative frameworks. There is a temptation to see architectural detailing as a process of bringing together standard solutions to familiar problems. As noted earlier, this tendency is promoted by construction technology books and through education where the typical detail is simply copied (and possibly adjusted slightly) to suit a particular need. While copying is one method of learning how to detail, it must be used in tandem with other, more critical and reflective methods. For designers in practice the prospect of detailing a building is anything but standard – the challenge comes with the joints and connections, especially when different materials, products and/or systems are connected to one another to create the whole.

Joining different pieces of the same material is usually relatively straightforward and has well-established fixing techniques, but it is a little unusual to assemble buildings exclusively from one material. When materials are combined numerous technical challenges are created, simply through the use of different materials in juxtaposition, e.g. attaching cladding to the structural framework and in doing so creating weatherproof joints capable of accommodating movement, yet impervious to the passage of water. The construction process is essentially one of assembling (fixing and fitting) parts together to form the whole. The interface of the parts will be via a 'joint' or a 'connection', that is, a joint solution.

Ultimately we want to know what a joint is in relation to 'why' it exists and 'how' it was made. Few artefacts are without some form of joint. The canoe from a hollowed out tree trunk is an exceptional example; there is only one component part, although a multi-jointed person is needed to make it work. Most other artefacts are, however, made up of two or more components. Taking a building as our artefact we find that it is made up of many thousands of components, the majority of which differ from their neighbours in terms of physical size, orientation and material composition. Putting two or more of these components together will create a joint and the manner in which this is detailed will influence the appearance and durability of the fabric. Our focus tends to be on the more prominent joints (for example, between brick wall and timber window) and control joints that are designed to accommodate movement within the structure. There are, however, many more, comparatively minor, joints that are equally vital to the overall integrity of the building and which require as much attention as the more prominent joint solutions.

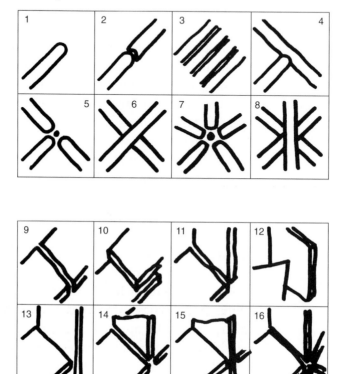

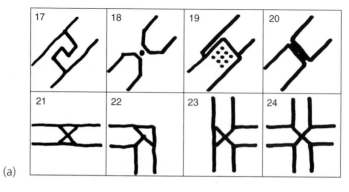

(a)

Fig. A3.2 (a–d) Fundamentals – how parts meet. Linear and flat building elements of different numbers can meet and join each other in different ways.

The number of components that meet will vary in number, may be of different sizes, made of different materials and will vary in their orientation towards one another (see Fig. A3.2). When the number of components, type of components and direction of components increase or vary, the complexity of the

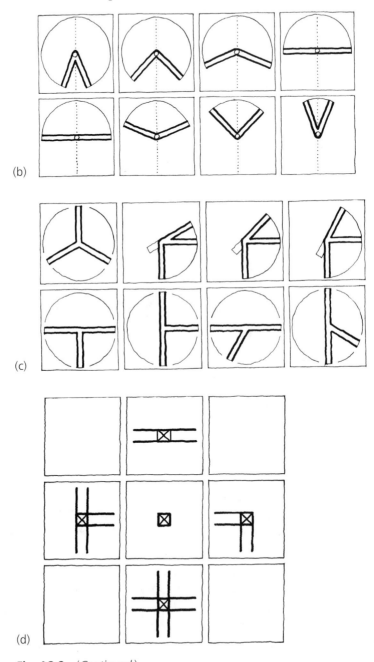

(b)

(c)

(d)

Fig. A3.2 *(Continued.)*

joint increases. In terms of simple solutions the best we can hope for is joints between identical components in the same plane. Vernacular architecture contains some very good examples of simplicity due to the avoidance of complex joints. The range of materials is limited as is the jointing method.

The complexity of the joint also depends upon its orientation, or position in the overall building assembly. Whether the solution is facing upwards or downwards, inwards or outwards, can make a big difference to its performance. The difference in orientation can be demonstrated with two very familiar solutions to the detailing of a roof. The 'A' frame ridge-joint has been used for centuries and is particularly good at shedding water and snow (see Fig. A3.2b). Turn the joint by 180 degrees and we get a valley-joint, a well-known cause of problems relating to moisture penetration because it is particularly good at collecting water, snow and debris (and often difficult to access for maintenance purposes).

Learning to detail

Truth lies in the detail, and the detail means complication, elaboration and doubt. Assuming that we had some time to think about our detailing and had the confidence to challenge the tried and tested solution, would our detailing be different? To answer that question we have to start at the beginning, by looking at how we learn to detail. As designers we are familiar with developing our conceptual designs from first principles, often drawing inspiration from the work of others, but careful not to copy their work (mindful of intellectual property rights and copyright law). When we get to the detail design stage, however, we appear to lose confidence and reach for a source of details that can be readily copied or imported into our drawings with minimal alteration. Too frequently the amount of time allocated to the detailing phase appears to be inadequate and so the task has to be completed quickly – in many cases without due thought or consideration for the consequences of our actions. The result is the promulgation of familiar ('safe') details, that may not necessarily be the best solution given our desire for a more environmentally sound approach to building construction, use and reuse. The more we rely on standard details as a matter of habit, the further we become detached from the technical issues being addressed and the greater the likelihood of inappropriate detailing.

We need to start by looking at what others have done (see Fig. A3.3). Fortunately both novice and experienced detailers are surrounded by sources of inspiration embedded in the

(a)

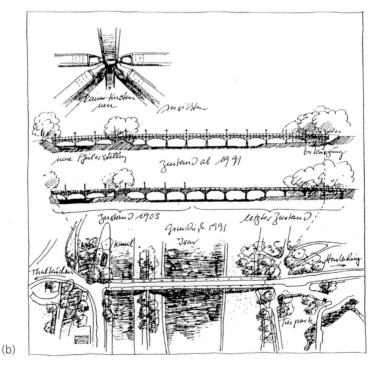

(b)

Fig. A3.3   (a,b) Bridges. There are many possibilities to bridge – to join – to connect – one side with another. However, joining in the whole as well as in detail is the essence of the construction of an edifice. (Courtesy of Richard J. Dietrich – used with permission.)

buildings in which we live, work and play. The secret is learning to observe and record the detail, and analyse our findings, possibly with the intention of applying that knowledge in our own detailing for our own designs. A sketchbook is an essential aid to recording details and notes, perhaps supported by photographs and video surveys. Maybe a laptop computer and digital camera provide a more appropriate way of recording our thoughts and our environment, but the traditional hand sketch keeps its own (special) value because of the physical (notorific) process of notation.

In addition to learning from what we see, as detailers we also have to develop the skill to imagine what lies behind the façade. In the majority of cases all, or most, of the building structure will be hidden by the building fabric and its finishes, a point also applicable to the building services. We need to make some assumptions based on our knowledge of building construction to try to understand what lies behind the surface finish and how it works as a building, for example, why does it defy gravity? We also need to read widely in order to develop our understanding of building construction and develop our skill for independent thought.

Typical questions that we need to address are:

- How was it constructed?
- What does the joint do functionally?
- What specialist skills were required?
- Is the relationship between the functional performance of the joint and the way it is constructed obvious?
- Has the detail weathered well?
- Is it easy to maintain?
- Will it be easy to replace (at the end of its design/service life)?
- If the building is to be demolished or remodelled, what materials can be recycled and how best can they be reused?

Learning from the past

Learning from the work of others is an essential learning tool. Our tutors usually direct us towards the famous designers/ engineers and well-publicised buildings and engineering projects as sources of best practice. These are important and inspirational sources, but so too is the more accessible work of less well-known designers and builders where excellent examples can also be found. Conversely, we also need to look closely at the examples of poor practice, the building and component failures from which we can learn how not to approach detailing, which of course is equally valid (see Fig. A3.9).

Learning from the masters

Well-known designers and engineers are a constant source of inspiration, but care is required because not all are so distinguished for the quality of their detailing. There are many examples of famous buildings that weathered badly, leak and/or are difficult to maintain and use, a point conveniently overlooked by authors and studio instructors alike. Indeed, we are particularly bad at returning to high-profile buildings and the work of high-profile designers to see how their buildings have weathered and how users perceive them. It can be very informative to keep a watching brief.

Learning from the ordinary

Well-known designers and engineers design only a small proportion of our building stock. Equally competent professionals who, for whatever reason, are less well-publicised, design the majority of our building stock. This is true of new buildings and particularly relevant to the alteration and adaptation of our existing buildings, which is undertaken by a wide variety of designers, builders and trades-people, often in a rather ad hoc manner. These 'more ordinary' buildings provide a wealth of experience embedded in the building, exhibiting both good and bad practice. As with the high-profile projects, these buildings are just as likely to leak, weather badly and be difficult to maintain if the detailing is poor. Such buildings surround us all and so they form a more accessible and equally valid base for our observations and reflection. The overall message has to be to get out and have a good look around.

Learning from construction sites

Few building designers build in a physical manner; they rely on others with different skills to implement their designs. As such it is difficult for individuals to learn from doing, instead we have to rely on watching others. With increased emphasis on site safety it has become more difficult to gain access to construction sites to watch work in progress. Often the watching has to be done from the relative safety of the site perimeter or the safety of the classroom via educational videos of the working methods. Observing materials and components being positioned and fixed in accordance with the design drawings can be fascinating and something all designers should endeavour to do on a regular basis. Observing how easy or difficult particular construction tasks are to carry out safely and efficiently provides essential knowledge for incorporation into the next project. Talking to the fixers and the fitters can provide valuable knowledge about the intricacies of construction that can be incorporated into our ongoing learning. Recording, analysing and reflecting on those observations is invaluable in developing our approach to detailing.

Learning in the design office

The design office is a constant learning environment. As novices we tend to learn by watching and copying the habits of other, more experienced, members of the office. Learning from a more experienced designer may be considered good practice, but how do we know that his or her approach is the most appropriate? Could there be a more environmentally sound alternative? Do we have the intellect to question (or even challenge) what we see all around us in the design office and on the construction site? From an environmental perspective the culture of copying may be inappropriate and arguably dangerous. If we are to address and hence reduce the environmental impact of the construction process and the resultant building we need to reassess how we design, detail, construct, use, reuse and recycle our built environment. To do so requires a thorough understanding of the underlying factors that bring about creative, functional and cost-effective detailing. We must constantly question how and why we detail buildings in the way we do, feeding this knowledge back into subsequent projects as part of a continual learning process.

The design office also offers opportunities to watch and reflect on how people work off site (for example, assembly factories and craft workshops) and on the building site through visits. Here we can witness a variety of issues, for example the parameters of manufacturing, packaging and delivery to site, the storage of components, how materials start to weather and respond to use (through condition surveys and systematic feedback mechanisms), and so on. By observing and questioning how buildings are constructed and have fared over time we are adding to and adjusting our practical knowledge base. The next time we detail we are in a better position to improve the quality of our work. Feedback and subsequent reflection are vital components in our drive for continual improvement, no matter how experienced we think we are.

Learning from doing at university or college

Education is the time to search, research and experiment. Design, engineering and construction organisations are concerned about liability and staying in business, and so learning through one's mistakes in practice is not encouraged. Time is limited and schedules must be met, so the detailing must be right first time. Furthermore, it may be difficult to find sufficient time to explore alternative approaches, simply because time costs money. With increased downward pressure on fees, and hence time, the approach of design and engineering organisations may be to stick to tried and tested solutions and not to innovate unless forced to do so. The same applies to contractors who may be reluctant to use new methods and products. During our education if we get it wrong the worst that can happen is that we get a poor grade for our work; no one gets sued or chastised for errors of judgement, no one loses their job, nor do we compromise the safety of others. If we have to spend some extra time sorting out a solution it is not so much of a problem, it is our own time and so missing a little sleep is not necessarily a major problem. One thing is certain, we will learn from the experience.

All students should be encouraged to experiment and push the boundaries to the limit; we may not get another chance. Academics have a responsibility to design educational programmes that are both interesting and informative for their students, developing the skills to think from first principles, learning to question and challenge conventional (conservative) wisdom and details (see sample exercises in Appendix 2). Essentially we are concerned with the development and refinement of transferable skills through the act of designing and detailing. When we enter employment our employers will expect us to be able to think, deal with unfamiliar situations and make effective decisions; this is what we are paid for. Having an understanding of first principles is fundamental to this aim.

(First) principles

Now we invite the reader to use his or her own critical and inventive faculties by going and looking around – making your own discoveries, forming your own opinions, observing things for yourself – instead of slavishly accepting or copying the usual solution. Through continual learning we are developing and refining our knowledge of architectural detailing, which encompasses both the principles and repertoire of joint solutions. We are also less likely to be lazy and rely on standard solutions. We have moved our thinking on, away from relying on information towards developing knowledge and applying it in a creative and practical manner.

When we start to become confident in recording and analysing the work of others we are then in a position to start thinking about detailing our own buildings. Drawing is an integral part of the design process. Our thinking in the way of associating performance with materials, size, shape and position, relating parts with the whole, is aided by the development of drawings. Whatever tool we use to draw and hence design, be it a brush, pencil, pen, computer cursor, etc., the tool should be a natural extension of our thinking. Thinking and drawing three-dimensionally is an essential skill to develop simply because the materials and components have shape and form. Details are three-dimensional objects that someone (with or without the help of tools) has to place in the correct position in the overall building assembly. It follows that an important skill is being able to visualise the components and details in our heads while designing. In particular, the ability to mentally construct the detail from the perspective of those charged with assembling the components can help with constructability and subsequent disassembly. Powerful object modelling software packages can go a long way in helping with the visualisation before confirmation of the joint solution (which, paradoxically, is usually represented two-dimensionally). Designers search out, assimilate, filter, order, reorder, define and redefine, make decisions and then present the information through a suitable medium, for example, drawings and written specifications. The end result of the detailing process from the designer's perspective is information that others will use. It is crucial, therefore, that we remember to consider the users of our information and their ability to 'read' and hence understand the message because it is they who will implement instructions and hence realise our design intent.

Neutral aspects

When detailing we can start with a list of aspects that are neutral to all situations (see Fig. A3.4).

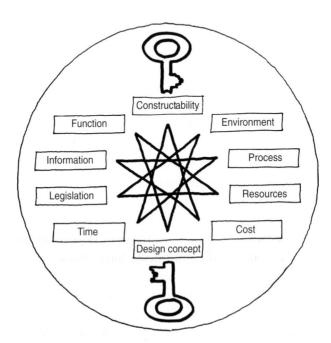

Fig. A3.4   Key aspects for detailing, both for choice and for integration.

- *Function:* The detail must satisfy the stated performance requirements; that is, it must be functional in use (e.g. durability, serviceability, user values, health and safety, and so on).

- *Constructability:* Must be practical and safe to construct, not pose a health hazard in use and also be safe to disassemble as and when the building is remodelled or demolished and recycled – method statements are required.

- *Resources:* Availability of labour, materials and technologies may differ between sites and type of project. This may influence the approach taken to the detailing and the construction strategy adopted.

- *Legislation:* Compliance with prevailing legislation is required, as is an awareness of national and international standards (e.g. ISOs). We need to recognise that legislation may act as an agent of change or, conversely, legislation may act to retain the status quo and hence limit innovation.

- *Cost:* Available finance and economic factors will influence the choice of materials and assembly. Life cycle costing techniques should be used throughout.

- *Time:* Time will influence the decisions made during the detailing phase and is linked to the financing of the project (professional fees = time).

- *Information:* Availability of information will affect the choices made by the designers as well as influencing the actions of those involved in production, use and reuse, and so on.

- *Process:* Scheduling and sequencing of production operations must be considered to enable safe and efficient production.

- *Design concept:* Ability to detail and enhance, rather than detract from, the original design concept which has been approved by client and legislative bodies (for example, town planners).

- *Environmental impact:* The solution will have an impact and this must be borne in mind when considering the factors listed above. Negative impacts must be avoided or at least minimised; positive impacts must be promoted and encouraged.

Now we can add some colour to our neutral aspects.

A green approach

Given the significant environmental impact of the construction process and in particular the use of buildings through their lifetime, our starting point must be founded on an environmental agenda (Fig. A3.5). The Greek word *oikos*, from which the word 'ecology' derives, not only covers the house and home (as a cave or nest) but also the surrounding environment that is necessary for the survival of a living being. Our planet, with its resources, creatures and their micro-environment, is able to survive without the actions of humans. The opposite is not the case; we need an environment rich in resources that we can harvest to enable us to survive (Fig. A3.6). The way we exploit our environment, the interaction between humans and our ecology, is (to state the obvious) a critical factor in our continued survival on this planet. Each time we build we make a mess of our environs, and that 'wound' needs time to heal. As designers and specifiers we can make a difference to the environmental impact of our buildings by taking steps to ensure that they are more responsive to communities, less wasteful of resources and less toxic to the environment. The philosophy behind *Agenda 21* is to think globally (that is, be aware of the bigger picture) and act locally

Fig. A3.5 A green approach means more than superficial green colouring. Green roofs and green elevations may be good, but they are not sufficient on their own for a comprehensive approach.

Fig. A3.6   Sharing the 'global cake'? Only 20% of humankind, the Rich, the technologically advanced countries of the First and Second Worlds, exploit, handle and consume 80% of the resources of the planet. And 80% of the world society, the Poor in the Third and Fourth Worlds, have to try to survive with only the remaining 20% of resources. Moreover 20% of the world population struggles to survive because of homelessness. Sustainable building has to be seen within this context.

(that is, source from the community and address context). Simply put, the main principles are that buildings should be:

- easy to assemble;
- easy to maintain;
- easy to disassemble and recycle;
- and have a minimal impact on the environment at all stages.

These are our first principles from which we can start to develop a list of performance requirements for specific designs and joint solutions. The desire to work towards a more environmentally friendly approach to construction requires a change in many of our established practices. It requires all of us to ask different questions with the aim of acquiring and applying new knowledge to the benefit of our built and natural environments.

A whole-life approach

Building on the need for a more responsible approach grounded in an understanding of ecological principles, we come to the issue of life cycle analysis and the whole-life costing approach to construction. Life cycle analysis (LCA) is starting to be used as a valuable and practical tool for implementing environmental policy in construction. LCA helps designers to address areas such as the use of resources, human health and ecology by seeking to expose the relative impacts of different building products (Fig. A3.7). Whole-life costing (a development of cost-in-use) is primarily concerned with project investment decisions, but there is a strong and pervasive argument for using whole-life costing as a design tool to support a greener approach to building. Early work in this field is starting to come to the conclusion that the biggest challenge concerns the interface between materials and components, the joint solution. Presently we lack reliable information from which to make realistic and meaningful decisions in relation to the interfaces; we need to develop a better understanding of how buildings react to use (Fig. A3.8). Regardless of this fact, the important point to make is that we need to take a longer, more integrated view of our built environment, a wider societal view of our built facilities and their effective management right through to recovery management. Our concern should be directed to flows of energy, materials, information, finance and people over the whole life of the building.

A performance approach

Another (strongly related) starting point is to develop a list of performance criteria that the detail must meet, known as a performance specification. For example, we could state our requirements for an external wall in terms of the internal and external finish required, the maximum and minimum load-bearing capacity, thermal insulation requirements, sound insulation, maintenance requirements, cost limits, recycling strategy, and so on. Essentially we are setting a series of parameters that have to be met (or bettered) by the designer, and subsequently the contractor.

Many detailers will be dealing with these issues anyway. Some of the performance requirements will be expressed explicitly in the client's requirements, some in regulations and codes and some in the collective knowledge of the office. At present it is unusual to find performance specifications for particular details, unless working on large projects. For small

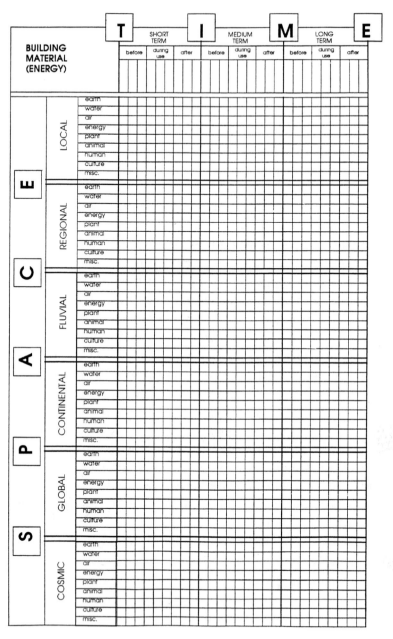

Fig. A3.7   Time and space: building activities, certainly in terms of use of material and energy, impact on the environment as well as on humans in time and space. We distinguish short-, medium- and long-term effects before (production), during (maintenance) and after (change, demolition) the actual building activities and the use of a building. Effects can also be recognised as a result of deterioration, pollution and exploitation on various scales from local up to global. Even the cosmos or orbit around us already shows some pollution. The areas or objects of influence are ground and soil (earth), waters, atmosphere (air) and energy resources, and within these life elements plants, animals, but also human beings and the cultural heritage. Enough to consider. Did we, perhaps, forget something? How do we bring these effects all together into the same picture?

BUILDING ACTIVITIES
ARE RESPONSIBLE
FOR

1/3

FOR
ECOLOGICAL DISASTER
AND
FOR

1/1

FOR
SICK BUILDING SYNDROME

Fig. A3.8 Keep in mind the negative contribution of building activities towards catastrophes in nature and culture. Building is responsible for one-third for all ecological disasters, but – of course – fully responsible for sick building syndrome.

Fig. A3.9 Examples from our built environment without consideration for nature or culture.

projects this approach can be rather cumbersome and time consuming, but should still be considered as an effective way of making us think and act differently. The International Council for Research and Innovation in Building and Construction (CIB; www.cibworld.nl) has been championing such an approach through the work of its performance-based building network (PeBBu).

A collaborative approach

Approaches based on alliances, partnering and supply chain integration are concerned with improving communication, knowledge transfer and the application of our collective knowledge to the benefit of the project and participating organisations. From the detailer's perspective it is impossible to know it all. It follows that it is necessary to work with others and this means that we must develop effective working relationships with the product manufacturers, other consultants and contractors, a collaborative approach based on inclusivity. In modern parlance these relationships are known as 'technology clusters' and have been shown to reduce waste through the integration and exploitation of knowledge. However formal the relationship, we need to consider three parties: manufacturers, other consultants, and contractors.

Working with manufacturers

It is important to work with manufacturers and artisans, thus incorporating their knowledge into the detailing process (and learning from them). Manufacturers of particular products and/or systems will know more about their products than the prospective detailer will. Likewise, craftspeople and artisans will have a large body of knowledge concerning the practical application of details on the building site or in the factory. This knowledge must be harvested. The secret is in knowing where to look and whom to ask. Manufacturers are often heavily involved in the detail design phase. Some services, such as the provision of typical details and product-specific specifications, are provided by manufacturers for 'free', thus helping to secure the specification of their particular product(s). Typical examples are drainage layout drawings, and door and ironmongery schedules, the cost of which is built into the cost of the products and services to be provided. By giving 'added value' the manufacturer is trying to lock the specifier into their product and hence exclude their competitors. In some respects developing relationships with a limited number of manufacturers can be beneficial and is at the heart of supply chain integration. By working together the chance of improving quality and reducing costs is increased, as is the possibility of improving the environmental credentials of the products being specified through gradual innovation. The problem with such relationships is that the designer tends to rely on familiar products and trusted manufacturers. There is no need (from the detailer's perspective) to search for alternatives, which can lead to complacency, which needs to be recognised and dealt with by the design manager. Combining a performance approach and continually looking for new organisations to work with can help to resolve complacency and retain an element of competition.

Other consultants

Collaborative arrangements need to be developed with other consultants (for example, structural engineers, service engineers) who possess different yet complementary knowledge and skills to the building designer. For example, it is well documented that the structural engineer's input early in the design phase can have considerable benefits for the detailing and the overall outcome of the project. Elegant solutions and the achievement of minimal construction need early consideration and benefit from a close working relationship between architect and structural engineer. The same argument holds for services, lighting, acoustics, landscape, and so on. Notable buildings are often characterised as much by their creative and innovative engineering solutions as their architecture. Formally constituted and informal working agreements can be effective in maximising the knowledge that is applied to specific design and construction projects. The most important point is to put together a group of people who can stimulate one another and hence produce innovative and practical solutions. Individual participants' competences, as well as the ability to work together and share knowledge, are a prime consideration here.

Contractors and specialist subcontractors

The detailing process is specific to a particular project and is concerned with producing information that others can use to build from. Off-site manufacturing, prefabrication and fast-tracking the construction process all combine to shift the emphasis for design decisions towards specialists. Therefore we need to consider the process from the perspective of the fitters, fixers and sealers. Early involvement through partnering and strategic alliances can help to unlock valuable knowledge at the conceptual stage, leading to better constructability and more sustainable solutions. Different contractual approaches are available and how these various participants are integrated within the project culture, and when, is a matter for a particular project. The key is to recognise that the majority of the specialist knowledge lies with the people involved in construction activities; harnessing this to improve the constructability and effectiveness of our detailing is a fundamental requirement. Thus the integration of design and construction is crucial.

Towards a framework

We have been dealing with issues that colour our decision-making process. Indeed, the general overview of issues addressed in this chapter points us in the direction of a framework to assist us with our detailed design decisions; that is, we need some guidance, and this is addressed in the next chapter.

A4 THE BASIC MODEL OF ARCHITECTURAL DETAILING

When we search for a framework to assist with our detail design thinking and decision-making we quickly become frustrated. Within the fields of architectural engineering and building technology we are unable to find much in the way of consistent advice – not in research literature, educational programmes or artistic endeavours – and we have to conclude that there is no clear structure for the discipline. Certainly there is no common understanding about a generally valid or even accepted structure that contains all of the relevant elements in a consistent arrangement. It would appear that building designers are left to develop their own idiosyncratic approach to detailing as they learn their profession through experiential learning.

A metaphysical journey

It might be that this missing 'anatomy' of the material or materialised side of architecture and building technology is also one of the reasons behind the fact that detailing takes second or third place after the 'great concept'. This is surprising given the widespread recognition of the importance, meaning and basic place of the detail in the whole. So, while we recognise that learning will take place in the creative environment of the design office, we recognise the need for a simple, yet practical, guide that students and practitioners can use. Here, we underline our plea for conceptual detailing and put forward the basic model of the architectural detail as a pragmatic and creative decision-support tool. Moving on from the philosophy of architectural detailing we now present an 'anatomy' of architectural engineering and building technology (Fig. A4.1). Once we understand the anatomy of the objects we deal with on a

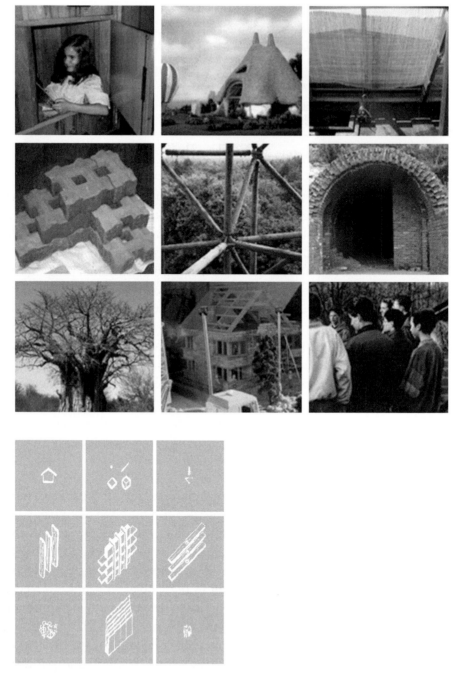

(a)

(b)

Fig. A4.1   The basics of the basic model. (a) Starting with the bottom right corner and going clockwise we see – 'human factors', 'natural environment', 'use or function', 'indoor climate' together 'with installations'. On the horizontal axis we have on the left-hand side 'building material and energy' and on the right-hand side 'building parts and components'. On the vertical axis we find 'production' below and 'shape' above. All factors come together in the centre, in the 'joint', reflecting the whole, repeated graphically in (b).

daily basis in practice we are then better placed to develop and continuously improve our culture of detailing. First, we need to go on a metaphysical journey.

The temple of initiation

For an introduction to the concept of the basic model of building technology and architectural design we would like to use a metaphor: that of initiation (Figs A4.2 and A4.3). The inspiration for this was taken from the way in which the highest priests and most probably the pharaohs of Egypt were initiated into the knowledge and the wisdom of the past. There was, apparently, a

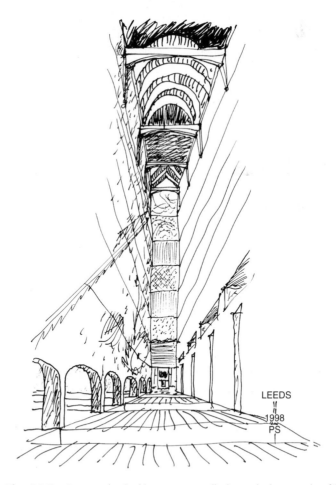

Fig. A4.2 A metaphysical journey: a walk through the temple of initiation into the secrets of designing and detailing, handling all-important factors, synthesising, co-ordinating, integrating towards a harmonious whole.

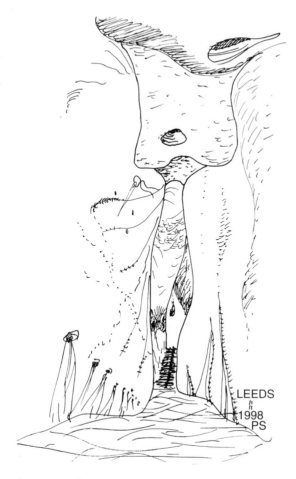

Fig. A4.3 The metaphysical journey continued: further steps in the temple of initiation into the secrets of designing and detailing with flexibility towards a dynamic equilibrium.

temple for initiation in Old Memphis which contained 22 images from which, following a long period of study, the novice had to gain the highest insights as the last stage of his education. Now follow us into the temple of building, technology and architectural detail for an insight into the elementary parts, their mutual relationships and their summation in the building whole.

We enter a huge building of three very high main storeys, which are carried on three large slabs and with the whole complex divided into compartments by equally large walls. All the surfaces are covered with information: pictures, figures, illustrations, explanations, calculations, and evaluations for quantitative and qualitative characteristics of all that is important and conditional in construction.

The floors

On the floor of the first storey is all that is needed to walk on, to stay on and to store things upon. Here are the more or less horizontal parts (including ramps), stair treads, platforms, terraces and the floors themselves with their coverings, together with all the necessary foundations – essentially a series of layers that may be applied in these 'horizontal' parts.

On the floor of the second storey we find all that is needed to build and to complete the structure around us, not only externally but also within. These are the more or less vertical parts and components like slabs and pillars or columns and all kinds of walls, including the important openings like windows and doors. Indeed, we probably entered the temple at this level through the first door of initiation.

On the floor of the third storey we explore everything about the buildings parts that are above us. We can also see them from underneath. These are the load-bearing, over-spanning structures, including vaults, cupolas, domes, floors with their ceilings and certainly all kinds of roofs, including openings such as skylights. In order to understand those components that are normally above us we are able to see them in mirrors as well.

During our journey we encounter three floors, which carry the three main categories of components and building parts: the ones on which we are walking, the others which are around us, and finally those which are covering the indoor space above.

The slabs

Three slabs illustrate all of the building materials that are available and these are ordered into three main categories. The first slab is made of inorganic materials, the minerals and metals. This very important group of building materials includes a vast range, from the earth itself (e.g. clay, unburned or burned, loam and mud) through stone to the metals. Everything mineral and metallic is contained within this slab.

The second slab is made of organic materials, derived from dead animals. Our first thoughts may suggest that there is not a great amount of this material in use; however, when we look more closely we find a vast range including, for example, sheep wool for insulation, silk covering, glue made from bones, animal skins (previously used for the tepee tent, nowadays for furniture). Everything derived from animals is contained within this slab.

The third slab is also made from organic material, but this one is derived from all available plant material. We find timber and wood-like material, grass and grass-like material including bamboo, plus cotton and hemp. Leaves, needles, bark, sawdust, rind and crust may also be used in the building process. Everything derived from plants is contained within this slab.

By studying the information on the slabs we will gain knowledge about the essential materials that are used for construction, those derived from natural and sustainable resources and those manufactured into component parts. We also find that all of the manufactured products available in the global market can be traced back to just three main categories of building materials: those coming from minerals, animals or plants.

The walls

Now we can go and look at the walls that are to be found in the temple of initiation. Here we learn about all the processes and methods with which (raw) materials can be transformed into components and building parts. There are only three types of methods or processes, namely: subtraction, addition and transformation (see Fig. A4.4).

First is the 'wall of subtraction'. Here we find the typical tools with which we can cut, saw, hack and bore. Although we start with simple instruments such as an axe and a handsaw we quickly progress to the most sophisticated machines operated and controlled by computer programs. Nevertheless all of them are concerned with taking away material, in one form or another.

Next is the 'wall of addition'. Typical tools here are those with which we can literally build up material, for example, a shovel or trowel. Hammers and screwdrivers have a similar function and belong to the simple tools. Again, these simple tools have become more sophisticated and more powerful, responding to advances in engineering; however, they all aim to aid the task of adding one material to another.

Finally we encounter the 'wall of transformation'. The tools typical for this method or process allow us to change the form or shape of a material without taking away or adding some material – at least in principle. From an amorphous form we shape a precise form, suitable for building. Originally we used our hands in order to give shape to a house; now many of these processes have been taken over by mechanisation, although we should remember that in some parts of the world human hands still do much of the building.

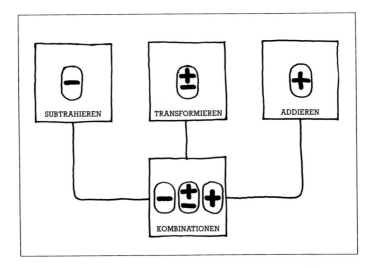

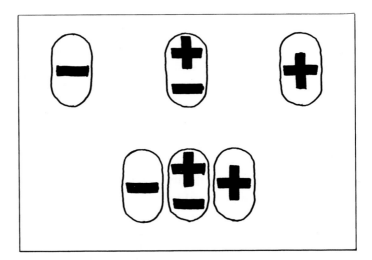

Fig. A4.4 Building and detailing means transformation. There are only a very few possibilities of transformation (addition, subtraction, transformation and a combination of them all).

Principles of processing

On the path of initiation we learn that these 'principles of processing' are already known in the ancient Indian culture. Subtraction was inherent in the principle of Shiva, the destroyer. Addition was connected with the principle of Brahma, the creator, and transformation was carried by the principle of Vishnu, the maintainer. However, at this juncture it is important to note that none of these principles appears in its pure form; they are always mixed, with one of them dominating or ruling the others. Translating these important principles to building technology in the light of a sustainable approach to construction, and also in the context of an unconscious but natural human-ecological way of 'house-keeping', we can observe the following:

(1) Whenever we take away material in order to reach a desirable, useful and beautiful form, the material taken away has to go somewhere or be transformed. This means it will be added somewhere else, unfortunately often as landfill waste, or transformed by, for example, burning. The point is that nothing can be thrown away. In a responsible building process there should be no waste at all, merely transformation of matter.

(2) Whenever we want to add material to something, we have to take it from elsewhere; and there we get to deal with subtraction. This means that we need to be aware of the impact of that removal, that is, is the supply finite or renewable?

(3) Finally, in a transformation process we need the material, which will be transformed – even within a recycling or reusing process. This material has to be taken or subtracted from somewhere, and added to somewhere else.

Looking at the initiation building in its whole we recognise its form as a building mass from outside, as well as its shape of the space from inside. One of the fascinating aspects of the beauty of this virtually real object can be experienced in the 'dynamic' of its forms and shapes. All of the floors, slabs and walls are, when carefully observed, found to be irregular, comprising straight, flat and curved elements of varying thickness and direction. We see a fantastic, miraculous object with all the contrasts of small and large rooms, here low, there high, here narrow, there wide. There is a whole symphony of (geometrical) points, lines, surfaces, solids and volumes, which can change their positions, their mutual relation and their quality in terms of being straight, flat, spherical and so on.

The temple has some other secrets. A deeper exploration shows a slightly hidden fourth floor; one that comes in and out of view. It is on this floor that we find the technical service installations and the equipment, which help to sustain life and comfort within the building.

Similarly, there is also a hidden fourth wall. This wall contains all possible combinations of methods or processes and their sophisticated development, including computer-aided manufacturing, automation and robotics. They are not categorised by the simple method of subtraction, addition and transformation, but belong to a complicated and sophisticated transformation of a higher order. An example would be a combination of methods within a complex manufacturing process which uses specialist knowledge (that is not available to all). There is also a fourth slab, which we can explore, that gives us information about the many combinations of materials in the vast range available to the designer. Finally, we see that each building is such a combination of elements.

In the future, maybe, there will be a metamorphosis of the whole temple in its space, shape and form, just fitting to the task we have to fulfil as designers or constructors, as architect or engineer – the realisation of a tectonic culture. As we absorb the information and knowledge from our metaphysical explorations we are on the way to developing the wisdom from which to make informed decisions about design and architectural detailing, a process of life-long learning. To do so we need a suitable framework, a simple tool, to help us to build and utilise our collective knowledge, and our tour of the temple provides the basic principles from which to develop a robust decision-making guide for designers.

The basic model

Keeping in mind the principles of subtraction, addition and transformation we are now able to consider the detailing process from first principles. Many models have been, and continue to be, developed with the express aim of helping the designer to make more informed and responsible decisions regarding ecological design. These models vary in their degree of complexity and in their relevance to specific tasks facing the designer, and we would encourage students to explore different models for themselves. Unfortunately, the majority of these models aim to provide information about relatively familiar and possibly inappropriate solutions to the detailing of buildings. The models may be helpful in providing information but they do not deal with the crucial conceptual issues that underlie the details, that is, the models do not encourage critical thinking. What is needed is a simple model (Fig. A4.5) that can be referred to throughout the design process, which is applicable to all those involved in building design, regardless of our particular circumstances and skills level, and is easy to use.

The model presented here provides a comprehensive yet elegant and simple guide that assists in the generation of ideas and information that can be used as a basis for the development of detailed solutions. The model also helps to bring together and hence integrate all essential factors. This model has been developed from theoretical and practical work. Earlier versions (the 'building joint model' and the 'building knot model') have been refined and feedback from users has been incorporated to

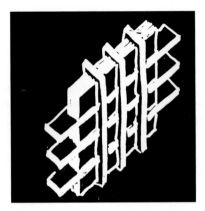

Fig. A4.5   The knot, the joint, the connection. A pictogram for the integration of all previously discussed factors. A (model of a) building itself – with the elementary columns, walls, floors – in a certain shape.

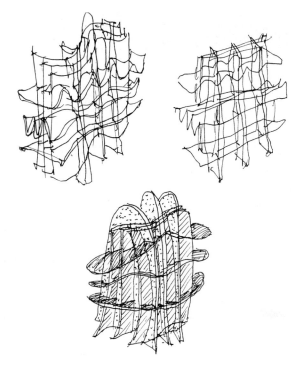

Fig. A4.6 Evolutionary and flexible. The centre of the basic model, the integration of all factors within the detail through the connection, joint and knot, can be shaped in many different forms based on possibilities, preferences and opportunities. This figure of the central cell illustrates some images of evolutionary, dynamic and flexible variants of shape.

make the model both simple and robust. The model (Fig. A4.7) fulfils various functions:

- It gives an 'anatomy' of the building (science, art and technology) with the focus on the 'nucleus' – the knot or joint solution.
- It helps to identify the most important factors that are conditional for the development of the design of the detail and its execution. It is also useful as an aid to learning.
- It is a base for further research and development. It is also a design aid that can help to co-ordinate the various factors, which can play a guiding role in the systematic collaboration and development surrounding the detail design phase.

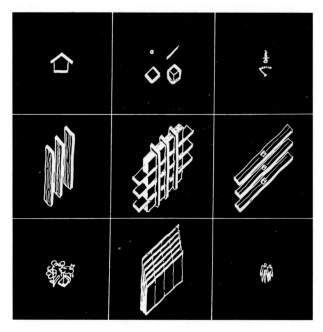

Fig. A4.7   The basic model for the architectural detail – an integral joint or knot model. The concept of the architectural 'nucleus' in which the whole of the building and the determining factors including human factors and environmental issues are inherent.

The model incorporates nine cells (see Fig. A4.7), which accommodate the following:

- *Central horizontal (material) axis*
  - left cell – matter and energy, the building materials (Chapter B1)
  - right cell – components and structure, the parts of the assembly (Chapter B2)
- *Central vertical (non-material) axis*
  - top cell – shape and form, the morphological factors (Chapter B3)
  - bottom cell – production and the process, the time factor (Chapter B4)
- *Top corners*
  - left cell – goal and function, the use of the building (Chapter B5)
  - right cell – indoor climate, the convenience within the building (Chapter B6)

- *Bottom corners*
  - left cell – nature and environment, the ecological factors (Chapter B7)
  - right cell – human health, the human factors (Chapter B8)
- *Centre*
  - connections, details, joints – the knot or nucleus, which is related to and reflected in the whole (Chapter B9)

Using the basic model

The model is simple to use. For each project the cells of the matrix are addressed, ideally as early as possible in the design process, but certainly for the design of each joint solution. The order in which the cells are addressed is a personal issue and tends to vary from designer to designer; it is important that each cell is considered in turn, and then returned to as the design ideas are tested and refined. Some designers start at the top left of the matrix and work clockwise; others may start with the corners or a certain axis. Our experience is that the process is iterative with the designer returning to different cells several times as a balanced solution is sought to the design problem to hand. Gifted designers may have a simultaneous view of all the phenomena described in the model. However, whatever our level of knowledge and skill the intention is to generate ideas and work towards more appropriate solutions to our building problems (see Fig. A4.8).

There is no 'correct' answer. The model is used to assist in the generation of creative design solutions to specific problems and unique projects. Each time the model is used the client brief and the building site will certainly be different to that which went before, as will the timescales, budgets, and so on. These factors will colour the decisions made by the participants and, of course, the outcome. It is important, therefore, to start with a clear matrix each time. We do not advocate reliance on using what was developed on a previous project (as is the case with many models available online), because this may well hinder the creative ideas we are trying to encourage through the use of the matrix.

Detail Design

Use Of Building	Shape & Form	Indoor Climate Convenience
A living space tailored to suit a writer, who uses it on a regular basis. An inspiring writing room will be the core design feature of the dwelling.	Ease of movement will be applied to space design. Access will be external, as the dwelling will be raised from the ground. Provisions will be made for all services within the layout.	Natural ventilation in all main areas. Heating Controls Insulated walls & Floors A warm calm ambience.
Matter, energy, materials Materials will reflect the site i.e. forest-timber construction. Man hours to cut, dry and prepare the timber for use on site.	**Nucleus the detail**	**Component Parts** Structural lumber, the factors to consider in constructing a timber dwelling. Dimension-This consists of rectangular cross sections, with nominal dimensions. Load bearing straw walls.
Nature Environment The dwelling will blend in with whatever environment it is exposed to. Wet Windy Cold	**Production, process, Time** Section made off site for speedy erection time. To provide a complete structure with ease of erection and manoeuvrability, with equivalent performance capability.	**Human factors** The dwelling will be tailored to suit the occupant, apart from the layout, which will be designed in accordance with the metric handbook. As not to discriminate against other people of differing shape to the writer.

(a)

Design Model

USE OF BUILDING.	SHAPE, FORM.	INDOOR CLIMATE, CONVENIENCE.
writer's retreat, basic, functional, ease of use, easy access between parts, William Shakespeare.	50m2, not boring, unusual (octagon), single storey, a retreat, The Globe.	comfortable, cosy, low traffic, ventilation (windows), heating, atmosphere for writing.
MATTER, ENERGY, MATERIALS. sustainable, timber frame, panels, straw, reclaimed stone/timber, insulation, natural materials, local materials.	**NUCLEUS. THE DETAIL.**	**COMPONENT PARTS.** panels bolted to timber frame, jigsaw, timber frame, stone foundations, straw roof, insulation.
NATURE, ENVIRONMENT. calm, no distractions, reclusive/alone, hermit, working environment, embodied energy.	**PRODUCTION, PROCESS, TIME.** panels off site/fixed to frame on site, bolts/dry joints, timber joints, modular, repetition of joints, prefabricated, reversible.	**HUMAN FACTORS.** one person dwelling, eat, sleep, write, wash, relax, ease of use, movement, texture, compact, visitors.

(b)

Fig. A4.8 (a,b) Examples of using the matrix. From student projects at Leeds Metropolitan University representing two different approaches to the same problem. (Used with permission.)

Reflections on the use of the model

Feedback from practitioners and students alike has suggested that the matrix should be used and reused throughout the entire design process. The basic model can be used at the briefing stage to generate ideas, which can then be discussed and honed to form the basis of the written brief that contains the primary performance criteria of the project (as illustrated in the *Green Guide to the Architect's Job Book*). Subsequent use of the model will start to home in on the detail and specific joint solutions, without losing sight of the client's overall requirements. But it does not stop there. The model has also been used to analyse alternative design solutions suggested by contractors and manufacturers while the building is being constructed.

A small sample of the many comments received as part of the feedback loop is provided below, not so much with the aim of convincing the reader to use the model but more as an indication of its uses.

Comments from three first-time users

- I was sceptical about using the model, it looked too obvious. Now I can see its potential, because it helped me to break down all of the issues involved in design and it certainly directed my final details.
- It made me think about my design from a different angle and 'think outside the box'. I found this to be a very useful tool in the development of ideas, concepts and processes.
- It helped me to understand why I was detailing, rather than just doing it.

Comments from two repeat users

- Once I got into the matrix I soon realised that this is a great tool for generating conceptual designs – if nothing else, it forces you to address difficult areas.
- The matrix is a useful tool because each requirement can be addressed and met through this matrix.

The basic model will retain its value regardless of changes in architectural fashions due to its simplicity and generic nature. The model can be used on many levels, for example:

- to develop an ecologically sound brief – the centre of the matrix becomes the brief;
- to generate ideas and conceptual designs – the centre becomes the building;
- to develop detailed design/joint solutions – the centre as the knot/the joint solution;
- to consider the implications of design changes – the centre as the knot/joint solution.

Summary

In order to champion the product it is necessary to develop a strong intellectual base grounded in an ethical approach and supported with generic and simple-to-use tools. From here it is possible to develop a deep, yet broad, understanding of our discipline from which real improvements can follow. Unfortunately, we are currently experiencing an obvious lack of a clear structure for architecture and building technologies. The basic anatomy of the field or branch of this elementary activity is missing. As a tool for orientation, recognition, judgement and development of design intent the basic model provides a primer for thinking a little differently and starting to develop new knowledge for the field.

We have to take into consideration the ecological impact of our building activity and, equally important, the health of the users during the life of the constructed works. We emphasise this once again because all contributors to the building process have a responsibility (we would argue, a moral responsibility) to pursue the high values in life and provide, to the best of our collective abilities, buildings that enhance the health and well-being of current and future generations. These essential factors are evident in the basic model. In other words we offer a contemporary and philosophical tool in the shape of the nine-cell matrix basic model of architectural detailing. The basic model is essentially a neural model that shows the anatomy of the detail in a 'nutshell.' In Part B we explore the issues and show more about the relationship between them.

Part B is presented in nine chapters, each representing a cell in the nine-cell matrix of the basic model of architectural detailing. Each chapter provides an overview of the main considerations for a particular issue (for example, human health), followed by some guidance and keywords which are designed to stimulate creative thinking rather than to provide all the answers. There is, by necessity, a degree of overlap between the cells, simply because it is difficult to separate out these issues without recognising the interdependency on other cells. We have also tried to keep Part B as holistic as possible while still being of practical use because to be too prescriptive would, of course, be somewhat self-defeating.

Part B
GUIDELINES

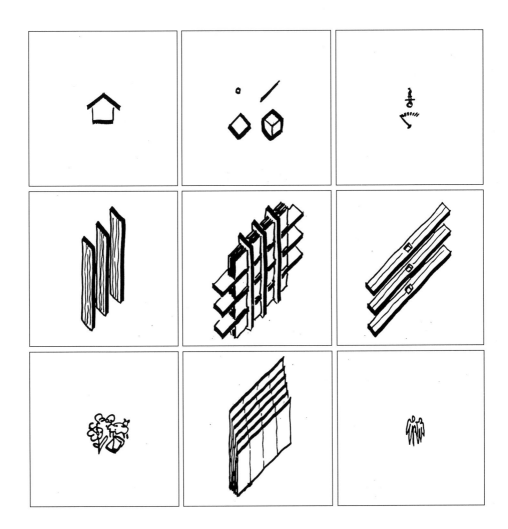

B1 MATERIALS AND ENERGY

Underlying issues

Matter and energy are two different expressions or manifestations of the same phenomenon. We cannot undertake building activity without using energy or material, and so we start with these two conditional factors (Fig. B1.1). We can also observe that material and energy are to a certain extent exchangeable in a building context, so that we have the concept of energy flow. In an environmental context we must make responsible decisions in relation to the materials and energy used throughout the entire life cycle of the building. It follows that we should recognise, respect and use materials and energy within an environmentally ethical framework. But finding guidance in this area is not particularly easy. We are awash with information related to sustainable construction, yet very little of this information

Fig. B1.1 Materials and energy pictogram. There are only a few main categories of building materials, deriving from (1) plants, (2) animals and (3) minerals, while energy can be seen as coming from (1) living beings, (2) fossil fuel, and, most important, (3) the sun – directly or indirectly.

will allow us to gain the specific knowledge we require. Take for example the challenge of adopting a whole-life approach, an area in which the theory is developing, but on a practical level it is very difficult to get the information about the environmental credentials of all materials and their related energy usage. So where do we start?

Not too long ago the choice of building materials was limited by the physical proximity of the site in relation to the materials and the availability of resources to work the raw materials. Processes tended to be very labour intensive and a lot of energy was required for acquiring and processing the material into a form suitable for building. Relative to their value, materials were expensive to transport long distances, and so choice was limited to local materials for the majority of the building stock, the exception being prestigious buildings. There was a certain economic, even ecological force at work simply through austerity. For many parts of the world this has changed. Now we can, and do, apply materials sourced from all over the globe, often at a cheaper capital cost than the materials available locally. The choice of raw materials and processed materials in the form of building products, components and systems is extensive. The 'cost' of this extended choice is to the environment in terms of pollution and in the worst cases the exploitation of people and societies through unethical practices. We should point out that we are not arguing for a Luddite approach to construction technology, rather we are trying to raise the specifier's awareness of the cost and consequences of the choices made.

A similar argument can be put for energy. In the majority of industrialised countries energy is cheap and there is little incentive to engage in energy-saving measures; instead we tend to rely on building codes and regulations to force us into designing and constructing buildings that have a more positive relationship to their immediate surroundings and exhibit positive rather than negative energy flows. From an environmental perspective building activity is expensive in terms of the energy consumed, but compared with the energy consumption of a building over its life this accounts for only 10–20% of all the energy consumed. Until we have moved to renewable energy sources our focus must be directed to minimising (or even eliminating) the use of energy from finite sources within our buildings. This is achievable in our new buildings, but it poses a considerable challenge for our existing building stock, which needs to be upgraded both in terms of the building envelope and the services within. We may need to implement more austere conditions with regard to the use of finite materials and finite energy sources.

Guidelines

It is useful to have a simple framework in which to work. Here we provide a very simple classification that may help to start us thinking about some of the fundamental issues from an ecological perspective (see material choice matrix, Fig. B1.4).

The main categories of building materials may be listed, starting with the most renewable materials and ending with the finite:

- plants;
- animals;
- minerals, including metals;
- mixed materials or composites.

We can also arrange materials in terms of the level of processing they experience, starting with the most natural and moving towards the most processed:

- materials that can be applied in their natural state, without or with very little processing;
- materials that are the product of handicraft and light industrial processes;
- materials that are the product of heavy industrial and energy-intensive processes;
- synthetic materials that are the result of a structural change in matter.

From this simple scale we can see that we need to try to select materials from the top of the scale and avoid those towards the bottom. It is also worth noting that experience has shown a marked increase in the risks to health from materials towards the bottom of the scale. In order to make choices we can use the material choice matrix (see Fig. B1.4).

Plant material

Biomass

The annual regrowth of biomass is a highly sustainable resource that is not exploited enough at present. The potential for new product development based on biomass is exciting and still to be exploited through the combination of new and old techniques. Some obvious examples (see Fig. B1.2) are:

- reed, straw and palm roof covering;
- pressed straw panels for walls and ceilings;
- straw bales for wall construction, flax for insulation, and so on;
- rice, grass and straw panels made by hand and/or machine;
- bamboo for load-bearing applications, e.g. scaffolding.

Wood

Wood can be shaped in many different ways with minimal waste. Assuming that we can source timber from forests that are managed in a responsible and sustainable manner, we have a material that can be used creatively, is load-bearing and has positive health benefits to building users.

Animal material

The use of animal material may be of the least importance quantitatively, but there is a strong tradition of using animal skins in construction (for example, tents and rugs) and bones for glue. Animal hair was at one time used as a reinforcement in mortar, is still woven for different types of fabric for use in buildings, and more recently has been reinvented for insulation (sheep's wool) (see Fig. B1.2).

Mineral material

Mineral materials are not renewable and so they should be used sparingly and also be designed for reuse and/or easy recovery when the building is disassembled or remodelled (see Fig. B1.3).

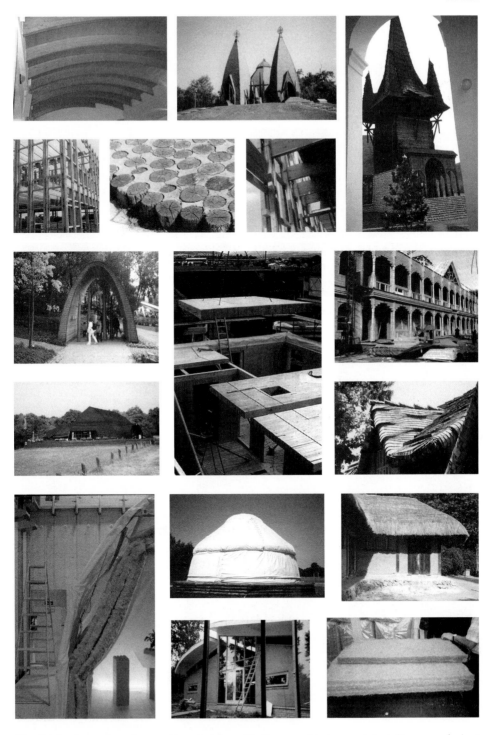

Fig. B1.2 Examples of organic material application considering sustainability: use of plant material (biomass), use of vegetation, use of timber/wood, use of animal material.

Fig. B1.3 Examples of inorganic material application considering sustainability: use of mineral material (clay, loam, mud, earth), use of mineral material (bricks), use of mineral material (stone), use of metals, derived from minerals, and recycled materials.

Earth

Clay, loam, mud or simply earth is the most fundamental of building materials. Mud bricks, earth sheltered housing are interesting approaches; there are creative options in conjunction with wood, and clay mixed with straw is another possibility.

Bricks

Burnt or fired bricks use a great deal of energy in their production, although they can be reused relatively easily if a lime mortar or a weak sand/cement mortar is used.

Stone

Stone takes a large amount of energy to process and good quality building stone is in short supply in many regions. Recycling is important. It is currently fashionable to use artificial stone, a cement-based product with stone particles giving the appearance of stone (best avoided, given the pollution created by cement production).

Glass

It would be unthinkable to build without glass, but its high embodied energy makes it necessary to recycle, and design buildings to exploit passive solar gain, thus helping to mitigate the energy used in production.

Metals

Given the high embodied energy associated with metals we need to use them wisely and always with a view to recycling and reuse.

Synthetic material

Synthetic materials are becoming more widely available in building and care is required in terms of their environmental and health impact. Avoidance where possible may be the most prudent course of action.

Being aware of the fundamental issues surrounding building material can aid the making of choices that improve health and wellbeing within them.

Energy

Energy is, in principle, a more simple issue to deal with. Finite resources must be avoided or at least minimised, both in production and in the use of the building. Renewable and clean sources must be utilised at all stages in production and use. The

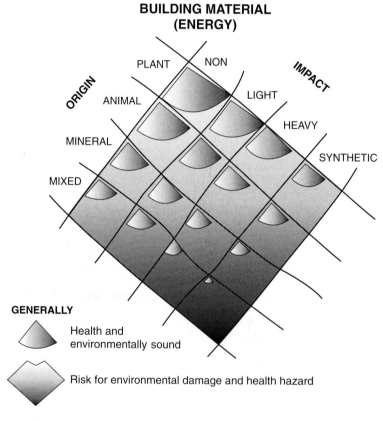

Fig. B1.4   Material choice matrix (MCM). Most buildings and building designs show a huge mixture of different building materials and components. The MCM can help to make a responsible choice between the many possibilities marketed to the decision-makers (designers and specifiers). The more we make a choice of a material in the lower part of the matrix, the greater the risk of environmental damage as well as health hazards. The more choices taken from the upper part of the matrix, the more chance we have generally to obtain healthy and environmentally sound results. Impact includes all treatment and handling (including energy content, transport, etc.) of a material, product component or building part from cradle to grave.

main problem here is that buildings tend to be placed in areas with existing infrastructure, and so the energy supplies are already in place and therefore determined by others. One way around this is to detail buildings to consume very little energy or no energy at all. To do this it is important to understand energy flow within buildings and the interactions of people with the building fabric and in turn with the external environment. At present we are preoccupied with reducing energy consumption (largely through better insulation), which is a relatively short-term problem. Once we switch fully to renewable resources (especially solar and wind power) the insulation values will be largely irrelevant and our detailing priorities will be different from what they are today.

Keywords

Design and service life
Durability
Energy
Environmental costs
Ethics
Health and wellbeing
Legislation
Pollution
Processing
Renewable

B2 BUILDING COMPONENTS AND STRUCTURE

Underlying issues

Closely linked to the choice of materials are the building structure and the manufactured building products that make up the whole (Fig. B2.1). In the technologically advanced countries we are overwhelmed by the extent of the choice available to us from which we have to select and then specify, trying to get the best product for the given project parameters. In areas where the choice is more limited we still have to get our selection correct, based on the information provided to us by manufacturers and independent testing authorities. Of course, it is difficult to determine which decisions were right or wrong, merely that with the benefit of hindsight some decisions turn out to be better than others.

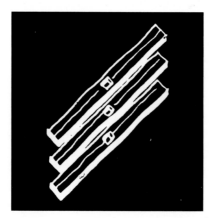

Fig. B2.1 Building components and structure pictogram. There are only a few structural components, forming a building and being connected: (1) those on which we walk, (2) those around us, and (3) those which are above us. All of them can have holes and openings with their own specialisms.

This selection process has to be conducted with the express aim of satisfying the client's requirements while also realising and enhancing the original design intent. The three-dimensional building object contains many component parts and building systems that are closely related to each other and to the whole. We tend to select products from manufacturers' catalogues, but we must not overlook the fact that we may want to create a new product to meet a specific demand.

Guidelines

There are two approaches to the selection of building components and structure, either via a performance specification or via a prescriptive specification. Performance specifications lay down specific criteria that the product has to meet (or exceed). The specification is written by the designer with the actual choice of product made by the contractor. Prescriptive specifications state the manufacturer and exact product to be used. The selection is made by the designer and confirmed in the written specification. The contractor is contractually bound to use the specified product unless there is a valid reason for requesting a change. There is no clear consensus as to which method is better; it depends upon the actual project. In the majority of situations it is common to find both performance and prescriptive specifications used; however, the recommended approach is to use performance specifications, thus allowing a degree of choice and hence competition.

Manufacturers, specialist suppliers, contractors and tradespeople hold valuable knowledge about their specific product or trade. It is essential that this knowledge be incorporated as early as possible within the design iterations. This may be via supply chain management, partnering and alliancing agreements and/or through the development of technology clusters, or it may be through very traditional procurement arrangements where informal relationships allow this exchange of knowledge – there is no one arrangement that is better than another, only that some are better suited than others to a particular set of circumstances. It is through close communication and co-operation with like-minded others that the possibility of adopting new solutions to familiar problems may be sought and explored. By approaching detailing from the conceptual level it is more likely that innovative solutions can be explored and new products brought to market through gradual or radical innovation.

From a physical perspective we need to distinguish between weight, load-bearing capabilities and equilibrium (see Fig. B2.2). (See Chapter B3 for morphological factors.) On a

(a)

(b)

(c)

Fig. B2.2 The main aspects of an often-applied building structure related to human capacities, sense organs and experiences. (a) Weight: the weight of a building or component is most important for its quality, e.g. for accumulation and certainly for the building process. (b) Carrying capacity: a building or a component can be carried, but has mostly to carry at least itself and often it has to be load-bearing. (c) Equilibrium: without equilibrium in a building component we can forget about success. A building structure has to fulfil the task of keeping in safe balance.

simplistic level, weight can be expressed as heavy (e.g. stone), medium (e.g. wood) and light (e.g. wool). The load-bearing capacity is concerned with dead load, live and imposed loads, and the material's need to be tensioned or stressed in some way. Equilibrium is concerned with the rigidity of the fixings, the degree of movement and the ease of disassembly.

From a human perspective we need to be aware of the qualities of building components and structure and the manner in which the combination of differing parts within a building is likely to affect us (see also Chapter B8). Perception will be via our sense organs (see Fig. B2.3), namely our eyes, ears, nose, skin, tongue and our sixth sense (extrasensory perception).

Our eyes are important in establishing our aesthetic judgements based on our perception of how our immediate built environment is composed. Here we are primarily concerned with form or shape, the quality of space and light, of solid and shadow. The morphology of shape and form relates to dimensions (scale and proportion) and to surface appearance (colour, texture, degree of transparency) as well as to the space between objects (see Chapter B3).

Our ears help us to distinguish between materials that absorb, reflect or transmit sound, which influences our degree of comfort within a space. Our nose helps us to distinguish between pleasant and unpleasant smells given off by building components; in some cases we may even be able to detect toxic materials or damp environments.

Smell also helps in determining taste, which we experience through our tongue. This is particularly important for young children, who tend to experience their environment via their mouth, hence the importance of specifying non-toxic products and finishes. The degree of comfort we experience from our environment is also perceived by our skin and directly by our touch. The quality of the surface finish of all exposed materials is important for our experience of the building from our direct touch and our perception of how a surface should feel, as is the relationship between temperature, humidity and ventilation. The manner in which building components are joined (e.g. loose or tight fitting) may affect the biological quality of the internal climate.

Our sixth sense is closely related to the health of the user, although rarely given the importance it deserves. Objects within

Fig. B2.3   Hearing: acoustical qualifications determine the quality of buildings significantly. How we feel within a room can be a question of its acoustic and, hand in hand with this, harmonious proportions. Nose: we should not underestimate smell or fragrance of a building or component, not only concerning ventilation but also in relation to the smell or fragrance of materials. Tongue: the smell or fragrance stimulates our taste experience, while children often like to lick surfaces, including whatever they can reach in the built environment. Skin: many buildings/components are touched or touchable, we also walk on some of them, we feel a cold or warm radiation, and often we see a texture, which gives us associations for a touch sensation. Eye: we see the buildings/components, what might belong to the most important experiences we can have from them. Sixth sense: it seems that the sixth sense played an important role in the past. Very subtle qualities can be recognised. We are on the way to re-exploring such qualities again.

our immediate environment may adversely affect some of us (perceived or not), for example, electrical fields, materials that retain static electricity, chemicals.

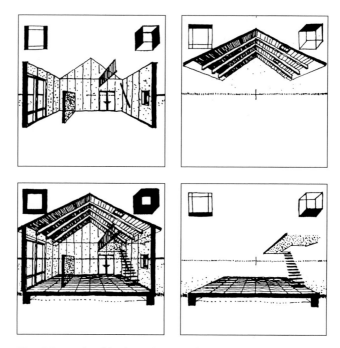

Fig. B2.4 Simplified catalogue of the structural components: approximately horizontally under us, approximately vertically around us, and generally above us. Each of the categories of components, beside their place in relation to the outside or inside area, has its own character, following the law of gravity.

Building components (see Fig. B2.4) give shape to the whole building and each component has to be judged in the light of its overall contribution to the building as a whole, its place and meaning. Creative and innovative solutions combined with gradual and incremental innovations in component design and manufacture will continually bring new products to the market. New product development is an important driver in the ability of designers to specify more environmentally friendly products. New product development must, therefore, embrace ecological principles at all stages of design, production, use and eventual recovery. Some countries have introduced legislation that makes the producer responsible for all waste associated with the products they produce, and so a recycling and recovery management strategy must be in place for building materials. Elsewhere manufacturers are starting to shift their emphasis towards a life care programme for their products and components, which should be encouraged by designers through careful specification decisions. What is certain is that we must not rely on our favourite products and manufacturers as a habit; rather we need to constantly look outside our current knowledge for information and knowledge about innovative approaches. Some may prove to be inappropriate, others may work out to be interesting and fruitful. If we do not look, we will never know.

Keywords

Constructability
Context
Health and safety
Integration
Interaction
Maintenance
Performance
Processing
Quality
Recovery management

B3 MORPHOLOGICAL FACTORS

Underlying issues

The morphology of shape and space is a prime consideration for designers and a discipline that takes a great deal of time to master. Here we are concerned with the power of shape and form, scale and proportion, gestalt, function and ecology. These are all factors that influence the efficiency of the building, its elegance in appearance as well as response to its context. The morphology is closely related to the amount and type of materials and components we use within the building. Morphology of shape and space will also determine the ease of assembly, ongoing maintenance and eventual replacement. It will also influence whether these operations can be conducted safely. Simply put, the joints and details rely on basic geometric elements of points, lines, planes and volumes (Fig. B3.1). The performance of our design solution will be determined by how we put these basic

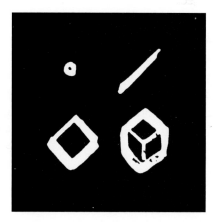

Fig. B3.1 Morphological factors pictogram. Morphological factors can be principally defined by (geometrical) points, lines (not only straight), planes (not only flat) and solids or volumes, eventually in all conceivable shapes.

elements together (see also Part C for examples) and hence how we create space within and around joints and buildings.

Materials can be shaped in such a way to be both visually exciting and structurally elegant – it's a case of understanding materials and the possibilities of structural engineering. For example, Eliado Dieste, an architect, engineer and contractor, has exploited this, applying know-how and creative thinking to produce innovative brickwork solutions, highlighting the unity between the joints and the whole morphology of shape and form. More organic approaches that draw inspiration from nature offer further possibilities; a good example is the Finnish architectural community which has a strong tradition of finding inspiration in natural surroundings and reflecting it in high-quality craftsmanship and building.

In order to benefit from a morphological approach to detailing there are some useful strategies and orders to be considered (see Fig. B3.2 and B3.3).

Points

A building and its details can be seen in its characteristic points. By points we refer to all crossings of two or more lines at a point. This point is mostly fixed and stable, sometimes flexible and dynamic, and the place where forces come together. So we could design by handling, managing and arranging the points.

Lines

Lines are the connections between points and come into existence where planes or surfaces meet. Again, planes are mostly stable although some, for example doors, are moveable. Lines create boundaries between neighbouring materials and components, which invariably need to be joined, fixed or sealed at the joint. Lines can also be places where forces meet.

Planes and surfaces

Planes and their attendant surfaces also give character to a building. Buildings and their details appear as a rich faceted body. Planes create and cover space and once again are places where forces interact.

Solids and volumes

To view a building and its details as an arrangement of volumes, solids and voids comes closest to the visible reality. With all geometric and ageometrical bodies their character is built up of points, lines and planes, which need considerable attention if the design is to function effectively. And this brings us on to issues of proportion and scale.

Proportion

In the context of morphology we need to deal with the phenomenon of proportion. Here we can learn from the past where various principles and systems have been developed, for example, the golden section. We are free to choose abstract and random patterns and/or highly repetitive elements as typified with standardised building components. Thus we develop a type of grid in which all points, lines, planes, surfaces, solids and volumes are present.

Scale

Scale tends to receive a lot of attention in design; it is an important factor in ensuring that our buildings are functional as well as attractive to look at. Obviously we tend to warm to buildings with a 'human' scale, i.e. one that we can easily relate to.

Guidelines

Here we need to be aware of the creative link between the overall concept for the building and the concept for the individual details in terms of helping to realise and enhance the concepts through the details (see Fig. B3.2). There will exist a relationship between the 'logical appearance' of the detail and the function to be fulfilled (see Fig. B3.3). There should also be a strong visual expression of the design philosophy, for example the expression of a natural and ecological solution. Do, for example, the proposed details enhance or detract from the overall design intent? Has the detailing enhanced the quality of the internal and external spaces, is everything functional, safe and a pleasure to use?

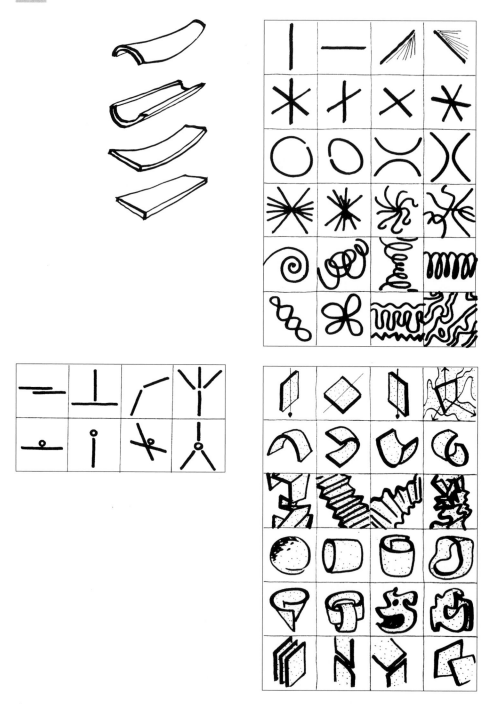

Fig. B3.2 Morphological elements, a kind of geometric alphabet, useful to be known and 'spoken' for application in architectural design – certainly for detailing. Points in various possible arrangements within the space – in relation with each other – developing lines. Some different types of lines, and some examples of how they can meet points or with each other – developing planes. Some different types of planes, and some examples of how they can meet with

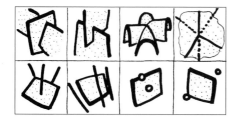

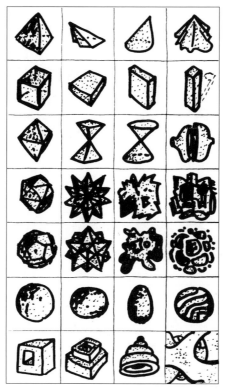

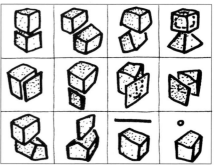

points, lines, or with each other – developing solids or volumes. Some different types of solids or volumes, and some examples of how they can meet with points, with planes or with each other. Geometrical elements can be stable or in movement. They also can visualise processes, happening in a certain time. Most important conclusion: all the lines and planes represent building components.

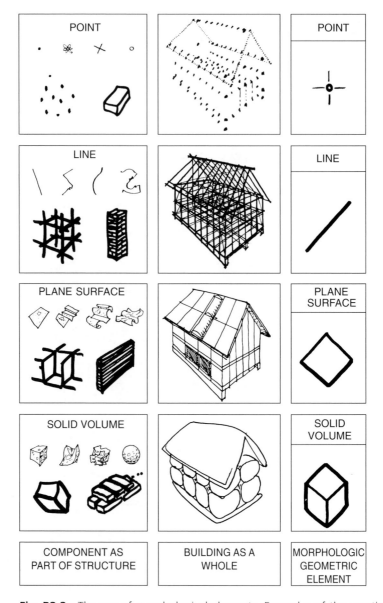

Fig. B3.3 The use of morphological elements. Examples of the practical use of morphological elements in design of the whole, its parts as well as its details, and also for their presentation.

Some of these questions can be addressed here as a means of generating information and ideas, to form the basis of our subsequent joint solutions.

Constructability and the associated science of disassembly form essential drivers in how materials and components relate to other parts of the assembly. All 'designers', from architects and technologists to engineers and manufacturers, through to the contractors, fixers and fitters, will determine the morphology of joints and hence the quality of space between them.

Keywords

Co-ordination
Ergonomics
Functionality
Geometry of elements
Harmony of the whole
Proportion
Scale
Shaping
Space
Tolerances

B4 PROCESS OF PRODUCTION

Underlying issues

When we look at the building process in its widest sense it becomes clear that it is a never-ending journey. Apart from the obvious design and construction phases the processes continue as the building is changed to reflect different user requirements, maintained, refurbished and upgraded (Fig. B4.1). It is only at the end of this journey that we become concerned with disposal via disassembly and recycling of materials and components. So the process of production needs to be seen within a whole-life context in which the initial realisation of the building is a short period compared with its overall lifespan. This must be recognised during conception to enable decisions to be made that assist and enhance the health of the finished structure as it ages, that is, we need to take a long-term view of

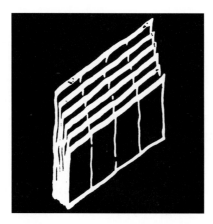

Fig. B4.1   The process of production pictogram. The process of production, shown in a few 'slides', representing the elementary methods of subtraction, addition and transformation.

the constructed works and adopt a whole-life approach to our building projects.

A thorough understanding of the various production processes, their limitations and potential will certainly assist us in the realisation of our ideas. This includes fundamental issues concerning the economics of production and programming of operations. Whatever our design approach, be it reliant on highly engineered components or craft-based techniques, we must fully understand the underlying processes before we are in any real position to produce effective details. Failure to do so will usually lead to wasted effort and wasted resources. It is this very knowledge that allows us to enhance constructability and make better progress in our desire for leaner construction and even minimal construction. It was Konrad Wachsmann who pointed out that it is the designer and maker of the tools and instruments of production who determines the resultant architecture in an age dominated by machine-made products, components and systems. It follows that the designer who is able to master production knowledge and is also able to make the connection between the mutual relationship of design and production will be in an ideal position to communicate efficiently with others who influence and shape production: an argument that also holds for an ecological approach in a digital age. Visits to production factories and artisans' workshops will help in our desire for a better understanding of production, and information technology can assist in knowledge transfer and integration.

In quantitative terms construction activities account for approximately one-third of our consumption of natural resources and energy. They are also directly and indirectly responsible for global exploitation, pollution and deterioration of our ecology. So we need to pay particular attention to issues concerning the life cycle of materials during design and production. Much effort is required for the transformation of raw material into products. After digging, cutting or collecting and transporting, we then need to get our raw material to one or more places to be processed. This includes cleaning and mixing with other materials, transforming, shaping and composing. More transport and temporary storage are often required between the various processing activities before our finished product is ready to be marketed. In many respects economic factors are at work here,

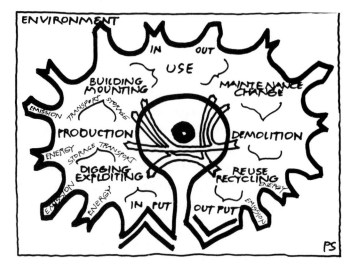

Fig. B4.2 Life cycle – the porcupine diagram. In the light of sustainable development we first have to look at the whole of a building process. In the diagram we see the entire building process with its use of materials – from cradle to grave or even from cradle to cradle – in its relation to the environment in terms of energy use and emission, between digging out of the environment (input) and bringing back into the environment (output). During this life cycle we face exploitation, pollution and deterioration of the environment. Partial reuse is always good, but it is only a very small compensation for the damage which the whole process causes. Because of the devastating effects of the life cycle of building materials the figure is called the porcupine diagram.

pushing and pulling the market without any real consideration for the environment. These processes are usually independent of, and detached from, user values and concerns at the other end of the production chain. Figure B4.2 illustrates the porcupine diagram, which attempts to show the repeated need for the input of energy and the output of emissions and pollution (represented by the spines). This is a holistic view of production, in which the relationship to the natural environment should be an integral part of the whole. For example, we could follow this line of thinking through to a conclusion that a building should be nothing more than a non-permanent compost heap.

Guidelines

There is a strong argument for increasing the amount of time spent on the design and planning phase of projects, with the aim of making savings during construction. The present situation, in which reduced professional fees combine with clients' desire to 'start on site' as quickly as possible, has resulted in a very short timescale from client briefing to start on site. It is becoming evident to those involved in building that this period has become so constrained that it is not possible to design, detail and plan building activities with any latitude for creative pursuits. The argument is that the more time is spent getting the design correct, the detailing perfect and the planning sequenced into safe and efficient packages of work, the less time is required to deal with uncertainty and problems while in the production phase. This does not need to cost more than the current system; instead, as with many of the issues outlined in this book, it needs a shift in our thinking and subsequent actions.

Design management literature and construction project management literature can provide some useful guidance in this area. So too can the growing body of facilities management work. All three subject areas (should) share a special relationship based on feedback between processes, thus helping to achieve a more integrated approach.

Here we need to remember the four essential kinds of processing:

- subtraction;
- addition;
- transformation;
- combination of the above.

Some tools for the processes are shown in Fig. B4.3. These principles can, for example, be applied to the theory and practice of lean design, constructability, lean and minimal construction techniques, etc. The aim should be to design out waste, design in efficiency and design in value (see Fig. B4.4).

Cost and project economy deserve a mention here. It is too easy to deal only with the initial cost of the project and ignore the cost of running and maintaining the building and the cost of demolition and materials recovery at some future date. Costs-in-use and the cost of materials recovery must be dealt with early in the briefing stage and at all stages in the production process.

Fig. B4.3 Tools to manage the various types of production and building processes. There are typical tools for the various typical methods for processing materials. For subtractive processes we have a saw or an axe. For additive processes we have a shovel or a trowel. For transformative processes we have a hammer or an anvil. Besides these we have various means finally for connections, such as threads, screws or glues.

Fig. B4.4 The building process simplified. The contribution one may give to architecture and our built environment is always conditional on the acts of materialisation and realisation.

Keywords

Efficiency
Integration
Occupational health
Pollution
Processing
Quality
Recycling
Time
Waste
Whole-life care

B5 GOALS AND PERFORMANCE

Underlying issues

It is the combined sum of the production processes that results in a constructed work, one that we use and abuse over a long period of time. We have to try to ensure a functional building that will not fail, either in its entirety or component parts, which is enjoyable and safe to use. The quality of the design, detailing and assembly process will determine this to a large extent, as will the manner in which it is maintained. It is an obvious statement to make, but we need to set goals and performance standards at the outset of the project, a task to be initiated through client briefing. The efficacy of the briefing (planning) process will have a major influence on the actions that follow. Here values are explored, which of course are different for the client and users, just as they are for those participating in the design and construction processes. So when setting goals and performance

Fig. B5.1 Goals and performance pictogram. The elementary symbol for creating of and being in a home, house or building shows the factor that has to be handled together with and supported by the art of detailing.

requirements care is needed to establish exactly which values are most important and to whom.

Goals and performance (Fig. B5.1) will be established during the briefing stage where the client's requirements and the anticipated needs of the building users are discussed, agreed and stipulated in the written brief. It follows that this cell also functions as an *aide memoire*, helping to keep the brief in mind during our more detailed design iterations. These overall goals and performance requirements will form the basis of specific requirements for building systems, components, products and joint solutions. The challenge is to communicate both the client and user values through the various iterations into performance requirements for the details. It is advisable, therefore, to address the goals and performance of details as early as possible, through a technical briefing document that can be used throughout the conceptual and detailed design stages.

Research and practical experience teach us that building users are never satisfied with their artificial environment for very long. We have examples of buildings that are perfectly sound and functional, yet have been demolished after only five years because they no longer fulfil the wishes and demands of the building users. This invariably liberates materials for reuse and recycling, and a quantity of waste material that has to be disposed of by incineration or landfill. It follows that we should seriously consider the durability of our designs and include as much flexibility as possible within the containers that we construct to allow for changing user demands. Such a goal will influence our design approach and in particular the manner in which joints are designed to enable flexible systems and alignments.

Guidelines

There are two kinds of relationship between the performance of the building and that of its details, either independent or dependent. Details may be independent of the type and use of building, for example the joints between bricks are the same wherever they happen to appear, be it in a house or a factory; they are generic details that all designers and builders should know and understand (see Fig. B5.2). Alternatively, details may

Fig. B5.2 A whole shelter/building and its specific but generic details. Remember the archetypical details and their inherent rules and you can check this example by bringing them into relation with each other.

be highly dependent upon the performance of a building and its use (see Fig. B5.3). For example, a laboratory building may require highly impervious joints that do not allow any transmission of contaminants. These details are developed in specific response to demanding performance requirements that are project specific. Performance requirements and project-specific goals will, therefore, influence our approach to detailing and our subsequent selection of materials and components to realise the stated objectives.

It is at the briefing stage where clients can be better informed and advised with regard to adopting a more environmentally friendly approach to the realisation and maintenance of the buildings they wish to procure and/or alter. Information about buildings in use is an essential component of a well-developed brief. User values (anticipated or known) are an important design generator. Post-occupancy evaluation techniques from similar projects can provide information to be fed back into future projects.

Fig. B5.3   Details are everywhere. Starting with the roof above our heads and recognising the preconditional details in rolling, swimming and flying 'houses', such as campers, mobile homes, ships, houseboats and even floating cities, all kinds of aircraft, spaceships and – to come back a little bit to nature – tree houses.

Keywords

Adaptability
Communications
Disability
Feedback
Flexibility
Performance
Time
Users
Values
Whole-life care

B6 INDOOR CLIMATE

Underlying issues

The inconvenience of cold and wet weather as seen from our indoor environment gives us a feeling of comfort (from a northern European perspective). We need a shelter from the unpredictable weather and in our desire to improve our comfort we have (with a few exceptions) isolated ourselves from our natural environment (Fig. B6.1). Our buildings are now sealed to prevent air leakage, insulated to protect us from the excesses of temperature, and detailed to resist the transfer of sound. The result is that we live in artificially created indoor climates, and given the amount of time that we spend in buildings it is vital that this climate is healthy and helps to promote wellbeing. Good indoor climates can help us to work and relax and provide users with high levels of satisfaction; poor climates have the reverse effect and sick building

Fig. B6.1 Indoor climate pictogram. Proper temperature and humidity, but also good light, good sound, fresh air and a clean atmosphere are all important qualities for the indoor climate which have to be fulfilled and supported by an adequate detailing.

syndrome (SBS) continues to be an issue for many building owners and users. We appear to be relatively tolerant of poor internal environments and continue to use buildings despite their poor quality. Sometimes of course we have little choice in the matter because we are 'forced' to live and/or work in such buildings. Awareness and sensitivity to our choice of materials, surface finishes, joint solutions, service installations and the mechanisms and systems to allow users to control their indoor climate are crucial to the creation of a quality environment. This is particularly true when designing for users with special needs, disabilities and illnesses. It is also quite a challenge for those concerned with upgrading the existing building stock.

Our fundamental aim is to provide a pleasant and healthy environment for building users, and a climate that building users have some control over (see Figs B6.2 and B6.3). Our main response, until very recently, has been to invest in highly mechanised systems that are controlled centrally and which tend to be very demanding in their use of energy. The user has little or no control over their immediate environment. With increased concern over air quality within buildings and our desire for solutions that are more environmentally friendly, we have started to move back towards systems that allow the user some or total control, supported by passive technologies. Computer-controlled 'smart' or 'intelligent' systems or manually operated (soft) systems are becoming more widespread. These are issues that must be discussed and agreed at the briefing stage, integrated within the conceptual design and then dealt with as part of the detailing agenda.

Guidelines

When it comes to designing the services and installations that contribute to and determine the quality of the internal space, we tend to experience a considerable amount of fragmentation of the project team. Lighting, electrics, telecommunications, acoustics, heating and cooling, ventilation and humidity, fire protection, security and so on are dealt with by specialist consultants. Each subject area demands specialisation, and the problem comes with the integration of these different areas into the overall building design. Many designers and equally many

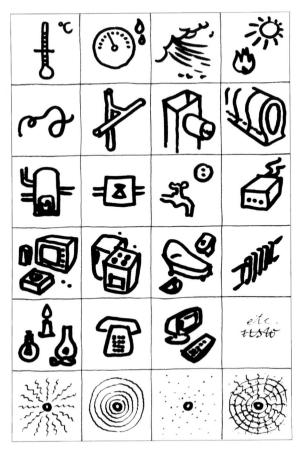

Fig. B6.2 Determining factors and how to translate them into building technology. The phenomena to be dealt with are temperature, humidity, air (to breathe, for sound and for freshness) and light. For transport we need cables or wires, mains or pipes, shafts or pits, wells or pipelines, and canals or sewerage systems. To create what we finally would like to enjoy indoors, there are several kinds of source, for example, heating or electricity plants. Often on the way a medium needs transformation in order to change temperature or tension of electricity. In order to obtain directly what we want, we need taps or plugs. Further, there are many types of objects in one way or another connected with one or other distribution (or collection) network, to serve our comfort, e.g. by cooling or by means of a vacuum cleaner. Sometimes our rooms are full of appliances. Space and connection are both important. Audio-visual equipment, appliances in the kitchen, bathroom, heating/cooling/air conditioning, artificial light, telephone, computer with all its inherent possibilities (i.e. embedded systems), and future developments in the indoor environment. Not to forget the effects of many kinds of convection, radiation and fields, all overlapping, together with the immense spread of portables and mobile apparatus. All these factors should be taken into consideration within our built environment.

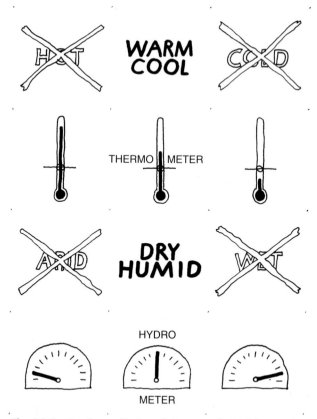

Fig. B6.3 For the wellbeing of the user of a building we have to strive for a medium quality, a balance, neither too narrow nor too wide: to prefer warm or cool between avoidable hot and cold, to prefer dry or humid between avoidable arid and wet, and so on.

specialist consultants know little about the other's field and are content to trust the judgement of others, who may be unable to question their proposals in any great detail. The result in many cases is poor co-ordination of the services with detailed design, resulting in abortive work, wasted materials and in the worst cases poor internal environments.

There is a strong argument for better integration of services and time to rethink how we accommodate the 'spaghetti phenomenon' of wires, pipes and channels to enable more flexibility within the container we build. Using clearly defined service zones is one approach, although experience has shown that these do not necessarily allow for complete flexibility in the way that we use the internal space. Again, the alteration and refurbishment sector is often restrained by the physical layout of buildings and so greater flexibility can be achieved only through relatively major alterations.

Taking into account the fact that the choice of material determines, to a large extent, the quality of the indoor climate, it is the responsibility of the detailers to make the best possible choices of materials, systems and installations and their connections. In the context of this book we would urge readers to consider passive systems and soft building technologies that allow control to stay in the hands of the user. Consider the window. This may be triple glazed to help the overall thermal insulation of the building, but it should be easy to open to allow ventilation when required. Simple shutters and curtains (see Fig. B6.4) are inexpensive, but deal with privacy and security. This is familiar

Fig. B6.4 Shutters, curtains and good insulation belong to the important measures or provisions for a comfortable indoor climate, which we call 'soft building technology'.

technology – we have used it for centuries, the only difference now being increased emphasis on the thermal performance of the window.

Keywords

Comfort
Ease of use
Energy flows
Health and wellbeing
Passive design
Performance
Pollution
Quality
Security
Soft systems

B7 ECOLOGICAL FACTORS

Underlying issues

Details, as the nuclei of a building, are a critical component in determining the ecological impact on our surroundings. The porcupine diagram (Fig. B7.1, previously Fig. B4.2) shows the relationship we develop between building activities and our environment, either an ecological imbalance or a dynamic ecological equilibrium. More specifically, the choice of our joint solutions and details will directly influence the way in which the building interacts with its immediate environment. For example, we tend to build to exclude our environment, but a more organic approach would be more inclusive and more responsive to our needs and of course to our milieu.

Ecological issues, our response to nature and our environment, are a major force for building and using buildings in a more responsible manner, a driver of innovation in both

Fig. B7.1 Ecological factors pictogram. Nature, the natural environment, is the base of our life and of all of our building activities. In a nutshell we define our environment in terms of earth, water, air and energy, plants, animals and also human beings and their cultural heritage.

process and product. However, a significant challenge is concerned with the availability of accurate and reliable information that allows comparisons to be made and decisions taken concerning environmental issues (see Fig. B7.2). A whole-life

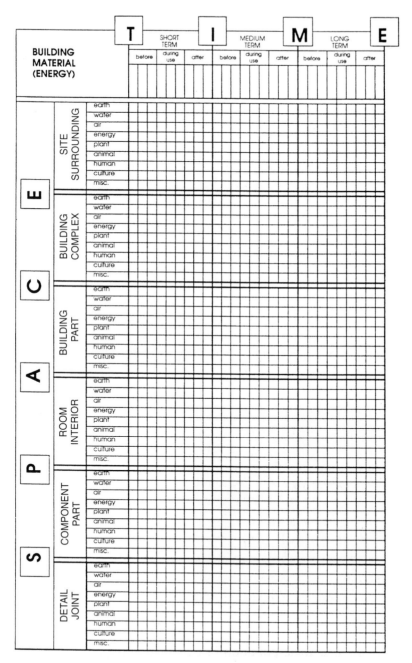

Fig. B7.2   A matrix as an instrument to check the impact of six items affecting health and environment in space and time: site, building complex, building part, room, component and detail.

approach is widely advocated, but it is difficult at present to access the information required to realise this ideal with any certainty. We simply do not know enough yet (although the evidence is all around us). Environmental legislation and recommendations in the form of ISOs provide essential guidance. However, we should be aiming to better prevailing legislation in terms of ecological factors (since legislation tends to follow best practice) if we really wish to push the boundaries and set a good example to others.

Guidelines

Construction activities have three primary effects on our natural environment that need to be recognised and addressed. They are deterioration, exploitation and pollution (see Fig. B7.3).

Deterioration

This means that we interfere with our environment through our construction activities. As long as the environment can recover from these intrusions within a relatively short time frame, in which no serious difficulties arise, we can design and build with a relatively clear conscience. Unfortunately, this is not always the case. But we should aim to complete our construction activities with a positive outcome in terms of our host, the planet.

Exploitation

We exploit resources, both finite and renewable. We must aim to do this in such a way as to leave enough resources for future generations so that they may meet their own needs in a responsible manner. We must make a conscious decision to use renewable and recycled materials and utilise renewable energy sources wherever possible.

Pollution

Waste and toxic pollution of our environment must be tackled. Nature provides a good example of how to avoid waste;

HIA
HEALTH IMPACT ASSESSMENT

AFFECTS EFFECTS

IN

AIR TIME SPACE **ENERGY**
SHORT TERM LOCALLY
LONG TERM GLOBALLY

EXPLOITATION DETERIORATION POLLUTION

ANIMAL **HUMAN**

PLANT **CULTURE**

EXPLOITATION DETERIORATION POLLUTION

DIRECT AND INDIRECT
EARTH EFFECTS AND SIDE-EFFECTS **WATER**
BEFORE - DURING - AFTER
BUILDING AND LIVING

AFFECTS EFFECTS

ENVIRONMENTAL IMPACT ASSESSMENT
EIA

Fig. B7.3 Environmental impact assessment (EIA). Here is a simple frame for a quick EIA check. The engaged or committed fields – water and earth, air and energy, plant and animal, human and culture – can be put into a list or a star diagram. By means of a simple scale between 'bad' and 'good' you can estimate the impact, eventually in maximum and minimum values, and you can easily see how the impact of the production and/or application of a building material, product, component, the use of energy, and the infill of a location can be characterised. The MCM can give some quick estimations.

somehow we need to try to imitate natural systems in such a way that the process of materialisation does not produce waste (see Fig. B7.3). This goes wider than just our detailing, but it is a principle we need to work to all the same. We should be able to reduce and eliminate toxic pollution with a little more thought during our selection process and with help from the manufacturing sector. The overall aim should be to leave the site in a better condition than we found it (Fig B7.4).

(a)

(b)

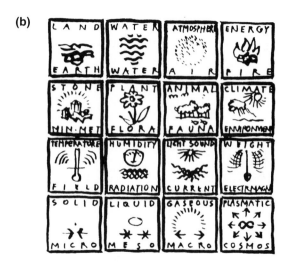

Fig. B7.4 (a) The house as an organism, interconnected with sun, wind and rain, with the ground, its temperature and underground water, with biomass and animals. Here we see the active and passive use of sun energy, a wind rotor, a (simple) heat pump beside a well, the accumulation of energy and insulated warm (or cold) water storage. (b) Ecological factors in a nutshell (from the metamodel of integral bio-logical architecture).

Keywords

Biodiversity
Deterioration
Ecological equilibrium
Environmentally friendly
Exploitation
Milieu
Pollution
Recyclability
Renewable
Waste

B8 HUMAN FACTORS

Underlying issues

A more ethical approach to the way in which we construct and use our built resources, where everyone on the planet has a right to a healthy and safe built environment, should be a primary driver (Fig. B8.1). The present situation is a huge imbalance between the rich and poor, witnessed internationally and locally within and between communities. On an organisational and individual level there is a limit to what we can achieve, but having an inclusive and fair approach to everything we undertake as part of our respective professions will, collectively, start to improve our built environment. We must adopt a more considered, inclusive approach to our detailing. With growing legislation regarding human health and safety, and areas associated with

Fig. B8.1 Human factors pictogram. Human beings are the reason for all building activities and the existence of buildings. That's common to more or less all races, all kinds of social, political, religious communities, all ages, all lifetimes, male and female. All are 'domesticated' beings, and therefore in the need of a (built) home.

disability, we have some guidelines, but more could and should be done. It is the detail design decisions that will influence the ease with which we can use our buildings and will therefore affect the quality of life of the building users. Functionality and quality of the spaces provided is a primary concern and conditional to our enjoyment of buildings and can directly help to reduce accidents within buildings and so improve occupational health. Greater attention to ergonomics, functionality and anthropometric data is an essential precondition to achieving a more inclusive environment (see Figs B8.2, B8.3 and B8.4).

Human (and humane) values may be different in different cultures. However, living in a multicultural society with

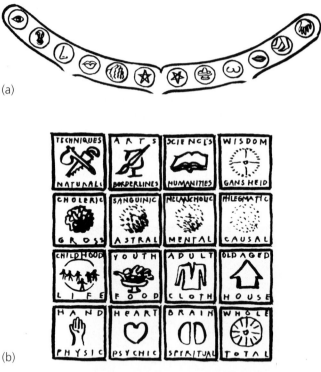

(a)

(b)

Fig. B8.2   (a) Our sense organs connect us with the world around us including the world of architectural details. On the one side we receive impressions through our eye, ear, nose, tongue, skin, and maybe even via a sixth sense. On the other side we shape and influence our whole natural and built environment including details. We build by the use of our fundamental active sense organs (and all their modern technical extensions), such as hands (to manipulate), feet (to move), mouth (to inform), and the need and ability to generate and materialise all the artefacts, and finally we are building by the impulses or drives, directed by our will. (b) Human factors in a nutshell (from the metamodel of integral biological architecture).

Fig. B8.3 The sixth sense, detailing. A field of interesting historical study and a challenge for the future, which has just begun.

HIA
HEALTH IMPACT ASSESSMENT

AFFECTS EFFECTS
IN

TIME   SPACE
AIR SHORT TERM LOCALLY **ENERGY**
LONG TERM GLOBALLY

EXPLOITATION DETERIORATION POLLUTION

ANIMAL   **HUMAN**

PLANT   **CULTURE**

EXPLOITATION DETERIORATION POLLUTION

DIRECT AND INDIRECT
EARTH EFFECTS AND SIDE-EFFECTS **WATER**
BEFORE - DURING - AFTER
BUILDING AND LIVING

AFFECTS EFFECTS

ENVIRONMENTAL IMPACT ASSESSMENT
EIA

Fig. B8.4 Health impact assessment (HIA). Here is a simple frame for a quick HIA check, with the same fields as the EIA. The difference is that for the EIA you estimate the disturbance of the eight fields by building activities, e.g. deterioration, exploitation, dying out of species, and so on, while for the HIA you estimate the degradation of the eight fields that are or become (by building activities) a danger for human beings, e.g. pollution, risk, uncertainty, etc. There is a high level of agreement between environmental and health impacts, and in fact they are inseparable. We only look once to the environment and once to our own health in order to sharpen our awareness of the important interrelations between our environment, our buildings and ourselves.

a growing tendency towards mutual integration, we should search for values that are valid for everyone. With a greater cultural mix it is our living and working environments, our built environment, which provide the places and spaces for cultural interaction. So, rather than create bland buildings that

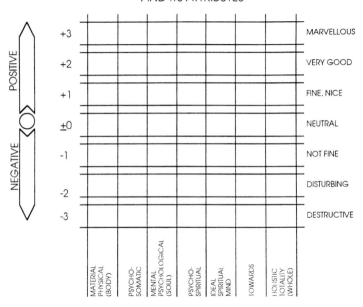

VALUES TOOL

AN INSTRUMENT
TO MEASURE QUALITIES
OF THE
BUILT ENVIRONMENT/SYSTEM
AND ITS ATTRIBUTES

Fig. B8.5(a) Human values – building and detailing is about the quality and value of life. Here you have a tool, an instrument to measure or to describe qualities of the built (and to-build) environment and its attributes, including the details. We qualify or judge consciously or unconsciously on physical, psychological and spiritual levels. We also know the fields in between (the transitions), namely psychosomatic and psycho-spiritual ones, and the total sum of all; the whole could be called a holistic qualification. Whatever you would like to judge or to qualify, alone or with others, such as clients, politicians, financiers, producers, suppliers, contractors – in a group or in a team – everything (product and process) within the building scene can be clarified in the light of what value it has (and for whom!). This value tool can be used for decision-making – individually or jointly, and for parts and details as well as for a whole, in our case, for a building. Nowadays our experiences with buildings can be judged not merely fine or not fine, but even (at the ends of the scale) marvellous or destructive (sick building syndrome).

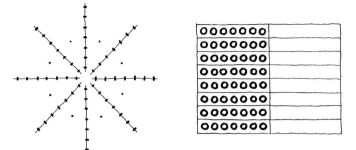

Fig. B8.5(b)   A star diagram can help to make the judgement clearly visible.

look the same wherever they happen to be placed in the world, we should embrace variety and let our buildings reflect their physical and social context. This statement follows from some basic ethics: truthfulness and honesty belong to the most essential social qualities, and truthfulness and honesty belong also to those values that generally get the broadest and highest appreciation in all cultures (see Fig. B8.5). Hence we should avoid the design and construction of a 'masonry lie', something that looks and seems different than it should be. In the broader context and in the depth of design, research and development, and education we can state that:

- a quantitative approach always has to be brought into balance with a qualitative one;
- systems should always be based on principles; and
- regulations have to be guided by values, not the other way round.

To capture the quality factors in relation to our detailing we have to consider all of the factors relating to our wellbeing. We have already established these factors in the previous cells, although it is here that their interface affects us most and is reflected in the details.

Guidelines

There are a number of issues we should consider here. Although many designers are sensitive to the issues highlighted below, we argue that everyone concerned in building should have a greater awareness of humane factors and make more of an effort to see these ideals through to completion.

Fair trade

As previously noted, we must take time to look at supply chains to determine the ethics of those involved if we are to eliminate or at least mitigate exploitation: this extends to health and safety issues. Our human values should extend beyond the artificial and temporary boundaries of the project.

Inclusion

Consider all users, regardless of physical or mental capacity and capabilities. None of us is 'average' and if we look deep enough we all have 'special needs'. As the designer we can make assumptions about the way in which people will use buildings; indeed, there is a considerable amount of literature and guidance available. (Consider user feedback, post-occupancy evaluation, and so on.)

Hygiene

Clean and hygienic production, assembly and disassembly processes should be designed into the details. Similarly, it must be possible to keep joints clean and hygienic without having to resort to toxic substances and/or unsafe working practices. Extending this argument we can see that the details must not be toxic in terms of the materials and means used and they must also help to exclude toxins entering the building while also facilitating the removal of toxins through controlled ventilation.

Ergonomics

Since we interact with many details on a daily basis, care must be taken not only in the selection of well-designed components but also in their careful positioning. Our senses of touch, sight, hearing, taste, scent and our sixth sense are crucial in determining our overall reaction to the space we find ourselves in. How we see and perceive our details, both directly and indirectly, is crucial; however, that does not mean that details must be emphasised or dramatised to achieve our goals. Meeting and hopefully bettering our performance requirements to achieve functionality should be sufficient. This applies to all design approaches.

Keywords

Context
Co-operation
Discrimination
Ethics
Fair trade
Inclusivity
Information
Occupational health
Trust
Values

B9 THE KNOT

Underlying issues

Working through the eight cells brings us towards the centre of the matrix, the knot or nucleus (Fig. B9.1). (If you have been working through the matrix you will have found it impossible not to consider the central cell.) So far we have dealt with eight interrelated areas that can be summarised as follows.

B1 We started with materials and energy, because without them nothing can be built, used and maintained.

B2 Building components and structural systems are then selected in order to realise design intent. This decision-making activity occupies a substantial amount of the designer's time.

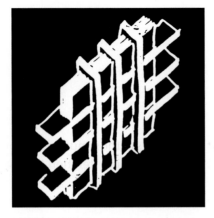

Fig. B9.1 The knot and the whole, pictogram. Everything comes together in the detail, the connection, the joint, the knot – reflecting the whole. And the whole (building) is based on its knots.

B3 Because all design has to deal with form and shape it is necessary to deal with the morphological factors and the possibilities to be realised.

B4 We must not forget the fundamental importance of the planning, production and building process, without which nothing will happen.

B5 The function or use of a building is the overriding reason to commence the design process. The project goals and required levels of performance need to be explored in relation to the users' needs and the characteristics of the site.

B6 If there were no strong desire for a comfortable indoor climate we most probably would not bother to build. Here we must consider the requirements of all building users in terms of the quality of their indoor environment in an attempt to enhance their quality of life.

B7 We must respect our planet and mitigate the effects of building activity, the way in which we use buildings and subsequently alter and then dispose of them. Ecological factors and environmental conditions are essential preconditions of all design and construction activity.

B8 Similarly, human factors are critical to the creation of exciting designs and buildings that are both functional and a pleasure to use. Respect for people and their environment lies at the heart of sustainable building design.

B9 Now we have explored the surrounding cells we are in a position to address the central cell of the matrix, the content of this chapter. Here we aim to combine, integrate, summarise and synthesise all of the issues that relate to the nucleus.

In Chapter A4 we visited the temple of initiation where we were able to contemplate its parts and their interrelationships. This experience is good preparation for the literal and figurative transfer of knowledge that we hope to achieve in this chapter. The relationship between cells is evident from our pictogram, which helps to remind us of the simultaneous presence of all the factors. It is through continual iteration that we revisit cells in an attempt to hone our design thinking and move towards the factors that will lead us to a solution. This design activity can take place on a number of levels, with the knot (see Figs B9.2 and B9.3) – the nucleus – forming the focus of the whole building, subsystems, whole details and parts of details.

Fig. B9.2 A knot example. A simple but moveable and dynamic knot.

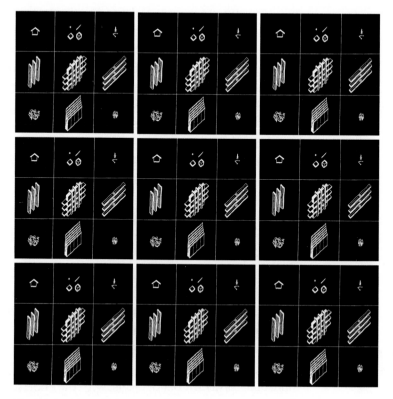

Fig. B9.3 The whole is more than the sum of the parts. The parts are not 'simply' added, summarised, but creatively integrated, synthesised.

Guidelines

Now the questions are concerned with what to do with the knowledge that we have generated in addressing the matrix. Although we have been engaged in the act of design by starting to turn our 'wicked problem' into something more manageable it is now that we are prepared to enter the famous 'black box' of design. It is here that we need the space and time to reflect, generate and test ideas in an attempt to reach a creative and innovative, yet practical and safe solution. While some of us may wish to wait for some form of divine inspiration, to be kissed by the Muse, to creatively ride on Pegasus, to be taken in the wings of Garuda – who knows what is possible? – most of us need to work within a tight time frame and so we need to work more systematically and force the opportunities for creativity.

Our decision-making matrix has helped in the conceptualisation and detailing of the building, in both its entirety and its details. The nine-cell model (Fig. B9.4) now contains notes, preliminary sketches and tentative proposals that can be developed further. In some respects we have developed a kind of protocol, which is beneficial as a tool to communicate with other designers and project participants. But it is also useful for inspiring the designer, acting as food for the black box.

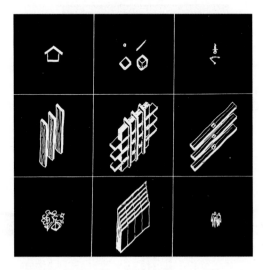

Fig. B9.4   The basic model. All the factors, in the form of pictograms in the nine boxes, together in the nine-cell matrix of the Basic Model. A matrix or pattern – together with the given knowledge – suitable for systematic detailing and an under layer – together with the various rules of thumb, given in this book – for proper decision-making.

Practical considerations and summary

Now that we have generated our initial thoughts it may be useful to make the material for the black box a little more transparent and goal orientated. This can be done as a group activity using, for example, the holistic participation method (see Chapter C5) in which the client, manufacturers and constructors can be involved, or it can be done on an individual level. Although we would urge a collaborative approach, we appreciate that in some circumstances decisions must be taken on an individual level. The process, however, is the same. Starting with cell B1 the ideas are reassessed against the conceptual design for the whole building as part of a final iteration, so that by the time we get to B9 we have the sum (or even more than the sum) of the parts. So B9 now represents a synergistic synopsis of all the partial concepts: architectural details within a whole, a whole (building) together with its details. Figures B9.5 and B9.7 repre-

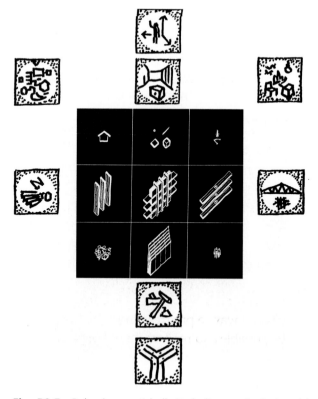

Fig. B9.5 Rules in a nutshell. Excluding ecological and human factors, which are not subject to design (generally already designed by nature), we give more guidelines for the seven factors which rightly are the subject of designing and detailing work.

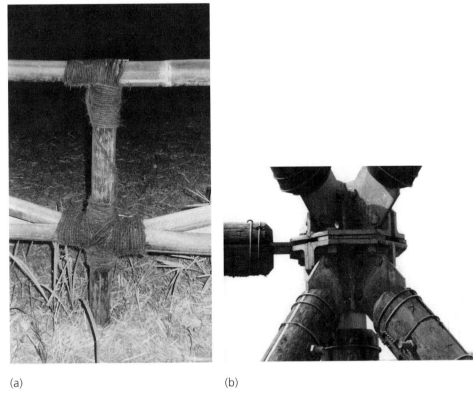

(a)   (b)

Fig. B9.6   Rules in practice in 'developing' and 'developed' parts of the world.

sent a graphic conclusion to this section, while Fig. B9.6 shows
a finished example.

Section B has been about generating ideas and information.
As noted earlier, the basic model is essentially a neural model,
which allows the user to start to identify pertinent issues, search
out and generate knowledge that can be used to develop joint
solutions for our buildings. To make ideas about building and
detailing operational we need to move into the area of developing and realising joints. A method for doing this is presented
in Section C. The hierarchical joint solution approach is one
(risky?) way to progress from the basic model (but others may
be possible and readers should pick their own way).

1. Location, Orientation, Use

Choose a healthy site, consider the orientation, optimise the function.

2. Space and Mass

Shape useful (closed or open) protecting space. Include identity and expression into the building mass.

3. Canon, Modular Co-ordination

Apply harmonious and ergonomical measures, in numbers, dimensions, weights – modular co-ordinated – eventually in a meaningful way.

4. Indoor Climate, Installation, Furnishing

Create a cosy and comfortable indoor climate with minimal installations and flexible equipment and furnishing in order to create a suitable atmosphere.

5. Structure and Construction

Design sheltering (load-carrying) structures and simple, understandable, durable constructions, which do not demand various kinds of means (e.g. elevators) because of their gigantic character.

6. Energy and Material

Use mainly durable, sustainable, endless (available/growing), easy reusable or recyclable, soft, clean, 'natural', energies and materials.

7. Production and Building Process

Produce in a humanly healthy way with a wise choice concerning handicraft or industry, selfhelp or automatisation and in co-operation and participation on all possible levels.

8. The Art of Joining

Join/connect/compose all building parts or elements in a harmonious way, rather solid, but demountable, simply efficient. Joints as nuclei determine (already) the whole.

Fig. B9.7   Conclusion. Rules for the eight components.

Part C
DEVELOPING ARCHITECTURAL DETAILS

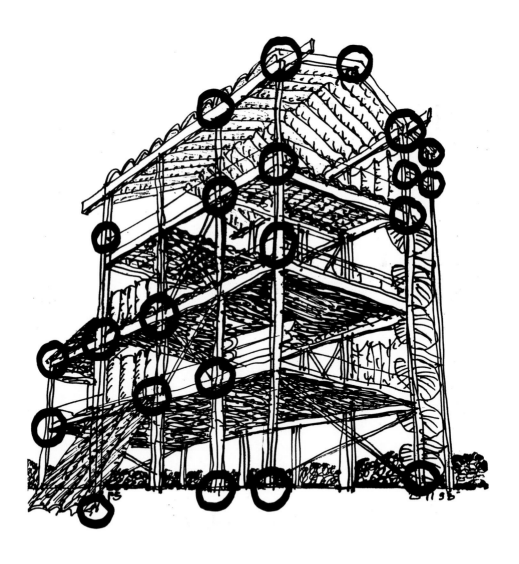

C1 DEVELOPING DETAILS AND JOINTS

Now that we are in a position to question how we detail, and have a robust decision-support tool to work with, it is possible to look at developing a typology of sustainable joint solutions. Working through Part B should have generated ideas and information that will serve to form the base of our detailed solutions. By way of an introduction to this part we start by looking again at why we need details and then at performance criteria that need to be achieved. From here we are then able to develop a more specific model that addresses ecological issues.

Introduction – why details?

Why details? To answer the question we can take the outer wall as an example to help to illustrate why we must distinguish different materials and products in building.

Let us assume that five factors – light, air, moisture, view and warmth – play a role in determining how the execution of the wall will be done. We will call these factors F1, F2, F3, F4 and F5. In theory the wall could be made of one intelligent material, being able to perform according to requirements stated for all five factors. This performance has to do with regulating, to a certain degree, the passage of light, air, moisture, view and warmth. We must keep in mind that these requirements are not static but dynamic, meaning that they change from one moment to another due to changes in environmental circumstances or changes in our own needs. Due to our limited knowledge and capability in building we cannot make a wall from one intelligent material (see Fig. C1.1).

Fig. C1.1

Let us represent the wall by showing five separate factor layers, illustrated in Fig. C1.2.

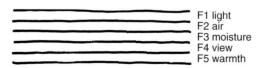

F1 light
F2 air
F3 moisture
F4 view
F5 warmth

Fig. C1.2

The first question we could ask is this: Is there a preferable sequence of these layers from outside to inside? We know from experience that we should stop the rain (moisture) on the outside (we do not wear a raincoat under our shirt!); we also know that we should not let the insulation (warmth) in our winter coat get wet. So we see that there is a specific sequence in the factor layers (see Fig. C1.3).

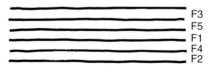

F3
F5
F1
F4
F2

Fig. C1.3

The second question could be: What are the possible building solutions for each factor? For each factor we can think of a building solution in the sense of choice of material and shape and size. We then can see that solutions can differ considerably (see Fig. C1.4).

Fig. C1.4

The third question could be: Which of the five building solutions could be combined in one building solution? We could now try to combine certain factors/their building solutions to one integrated solution. This will not be possible, as we have seen, for all solutions. The end result would be a wall with differentiated building solutions, considered in the depth of the wall (the layers) as well as in the length of the wall (see Fig. C1.5).

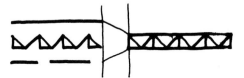

Fig. C1.5

Between all these different solutions, expressed by different materials, we will have joints, defined as discontinuity of material. Material as such can be solid, liquid or gas (for example, air). This also means that, strictly speaking, all surfaces of objects or parts are joint situations due to the fact that there is a change of material, for example, from wood to air.

In this simplistic way we have tried to show why joints or building details exist. Now we can ask further questions such as: How many joints do we want or need? How many different joints do we want or need?

Joints

In physics space is everywhere and continuous, time is constant and continuous, matter/energy is everywhere, but is not continuous. Matter changes, from gas to solid or liquid, from one kind of gas to another, and so on. Following this argument we can view a joint in a building as a place where matter changes. Take, for example, the humble window. A timber window casement in a timber window-frame results in a joint, simply because there is air between the two. A cross-section through the joint gives us a wood–air–wood section. If the window has been painted then our joint is more intricate; the joint section now comprises wood–paint–air–paint–wood. Add a little water penetration to the joint and things become more complex still. By definition all surfaces are joints between some kind of solid and gas, or solid and liquid, or liquid and gas. The next rather obvious observation is that buildings must therefore be dynamic, living structures that move to accommodate changes in temperature and loading and breathe to expel moisture-laden air. This is where the joint takes on a central and determining role. So our answer to the question is that a joint is a situation where there is discontinuity of matter within the continuity of space and time. This situation results in parts whose performance, based on the nature of their relationships, must satisfy various factor requirements.

We tend to view buildings as static structures that suddenly exhibit signs of distress, which need urgent repair. In reality a building is anything but static: it moves to accommodate changes in temperature or humidity, it flexes to accommodate increased or decreased loading, and it has to breathe to expel moisture-laden air if condensation is to be avoided. As designers we must recognise such characteristics in our detailing and choice of materials. If we do not allow for thermal expansion and subsequent contraction then materials will exhibit stress and will eventually fail; if we do not allow for increased loads the structure may fail; and if we do not allow the building to breathe we will have serious problems with condensation and the health of the user will be affected. If we view a building as a living, dynamic structure we may be in a better position to understand its maintenance requirements and, therefore, enhance the durability of the structure. We may also be in a position to better understand ecological issues associated with building construction. Construction is essentially a process of assembling disparate parts to form the completed building. The interface of the parts will be via a 'joint' or a 'connection'. A joint is the term used to describe the space between components; where these components are joined structurally it is referred to as a connection.

Putting two or more individual parts together will create a joint and the manner in which this is detailed – the joint solution – will influence the appearance, performance and durability of the total building. It will also influence the disassembly strategy for the building.

Control joints

Movement within and between different parts of the building can be substantial and can involve large forces. Control joints, sometimes described as 'movement joints' or 'expansion joints', are designed to accommodate movement and the associated stresses. It is during the detailing phase that materials and components should be analysed for their potential to move in conjunction with others and with respect to the overall physical geometry of the building. Failure to position control joints correctly and/or failure to size and detail control joints in an appropriate manner may lead to failure at a future date.

Connections

The word 'connection' implies some form of physical joint between two or more parts (see Fig. C1.6). The manner in which these parts are connected will be influenced by the materials to be connected, the resources available (human labour, tools and mechanical plant) and the manner in which the joint solution has been detailed. Care is required to ensure that the connection can be achieved safely and that future access for repair and maintenance can also be carried out safely. Add to this requirement the ecological performance of the connection and we need to consider forms of connection that can be disassembled easily and with minimal damage to individual components. Thus screws and bolts, for example, are preferable forms of connection to nails, glues and mastics.

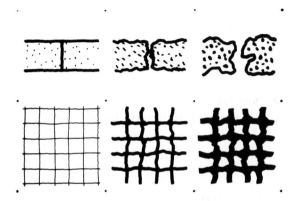

Fig. C1.6   Connections – the possible meeting of parts.

Tolerances

In order to be able to place individual parts in juxtaposition with other parts of the assembly a certain amount of dimensional tolerance is required (see Fig. C1.7). Construction involves the use of labour, either remote from the site in a factory or workshop, or on site, but always in combination. Designers must consider all those who are expected to assemble the various parts physically into a whole, including those responsible for servicing and replacing parts in the future, so that workers can carry out their tasks safely and comfortably.

With traditional construction the craftsmen would deal with tolerances as part of their craft, applying their knowledge and skill to trim, cut, fit and adjust materials on site to create the desired effect. In contrast, where materials are manufactured under carefully controlled conditions in a factory or workshop and brought to site for assembly, the manufacturer, designer and contractor must be confident that the component parts will fit together since there is no scope to make adjustments to the manufactured components. Provision for variation in materials, manufacturing and positioning is achieved by specifying allowable tolerances. Too small a tolerance and it may be impossible to move components into position on site, resulting in some form of damage; too large a tolerance will necessitate a degree of 'bodging' on site to fill the gap – for practical and economic reasons both situations must be avoided. There are three interrelated tolerances that the designer must specify, which are related specifically to the choice of material(s).

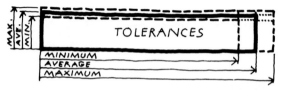

Fig. C1.7 Tolerances are needed not only between persons but between different parts of materials, elements or components. Measures are dependent on the possible exactness with which those pieces can be produced and/or assembled (see also Fig. C1.6).

Manufacturing tolerances

Manufacturing tolerances limit the dimensional deviation in the manufacture of components. They may be set by a standard (for example, ISO), by a manufacturer, and/or the design team. Some manufacturers are able to manufacture to tighter tolerances than those defined in the current standards. Some designers may require a greater degree of tolerance than that normally supplied, for which there may well be a cost to cover additional tooling and quality control in the factory.

Positional tolerances

Minimum and maximum allowable tolerances are essential for convenience and safety of assembly; however, whether the tolerances are met on site will depend upon the skills of those doing the setting out, the technology employed to erect and position components, and the quality of supervision.

Joint tolerances

Joint tolerances will be determined by a combination of the performance requirements of the joint solution and the aesthetic requirements of the designer. Functional requirements will be determined through the materials and technologies employed (see below). Aesthetic requirements will be determined by building traditions, architectural fashion and the designer's own idiosyncrasies.

As a general rule the smaller (or closer) the tolerance, the greater the manufacturing costs and the greater the time for assembly and associated costs. Help in determining the most suitable degree of tolerance can be found in technical literature provided by trade associations and manufacturers.

Dimensional co-ordination

Once the tolerances are known and understood in relation to the overall building design it is possible to compose the drawings and details that show the building assembly. Dimensional co-ordination is important to ensure that the multitude of components fit together correctly, thus ensuring smooth operations on site and the avoidance of needless waste through unnecessary cutting. A modular approach may be useful, although this may not necessarily accord with a more organic design approach.

The performance of joints

Now that we have determined that joints result from discontinuity of matter, the next question we need to address is: Why is this discontinuity necessary? The answer lies in building performance. For example, when we consider our requirements for an exterior wall, we want absolutely no rain coming in (moisture), but we do want an adequate amount of daylight (light) and a view to a certain degree from the inside, but less from the outside. To achieve the appropriate performance requirements simultaneously we must differentiate between various materials and products (brick, wood, glass and so on) in the exterior wall. By definition this action results in joints between components and also between materials. Furthermore it is not technically possible to fabricate one large brick for the whole wall, so we must produce smaller bricks, that we bind together by using mortar, and again we have joints (execution).

Once we have accepted the fact that discontinuity of material results in joints, we could ask ourselves what we should expect of joints in terms of performance. This is not an easy issue to deal with because it is difficult to identify the exact nature of a joint's 'performance'. Where individual parts come together at a particular joint in a building, certain performance criteria must be achieved. These criteria are threefold:

- *Meeting of parts:* the degree of geometrical nearness. The fact that parts are 'related' has first of all to do with 'nearness'. This nearness, being weak or strong, depends on the position of parts, hereby including the distance to one another, in relation to the size and shapes of parts. The meeting of parts is a performance of a joint (see Fig. C1.8).
- *Fixing of parts:* the degree to which parts restrict the freedom of movement of other parts. Once parts meet as desired, we would like to sustain this for a period of time. Parts can restrict each other's movement, specifically or absolutely. The fixing of parts is a performance of a joint (see Fig. C1.9).

■ *Sealing between parts:* the degree to which the passage of matter or information is controlled. As we have seen, functional continuity might be desired, even though there are joints. For example, controlling the passage of air is a function that must also be performed by the joint. The sealing between parts is a performance of a joint (see Fig. C1.10).

An interesting and vital question here would be: Do we need additional jointing parts, next to the main parts, in order to meet requirements considering the performance of meeting, fixing and sealing? And are there more than three performance criteria?

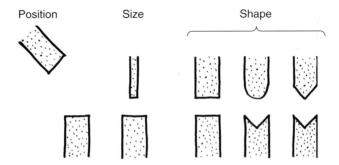

Fig. C1.8 Meeting of parts.

Fig. C1.9 Fixing of parts.

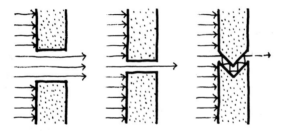

Fig. C1.10 Sealing between parts.

The general building model

In the basic model of the detail, three cells (see Fig. C1.11) are chosen to construct another model, namely B7 (ecological factors), B8 (human factors) and B9 (the knot). Here they are called ecology, demand and solution as the three systems in the general building model (see Fig. C1.12).

Whereas the basic model of the detail (Part B) more or less resembles a neural matrix that can be used as a meditative checklist while developing joints and details, the general building model is a more specific model in order to be more operational in the process of developing joints. It must be noted that what follows from here is a way, and not 'the' way, to reason about and hence develop joints; other approaches may also be valid.

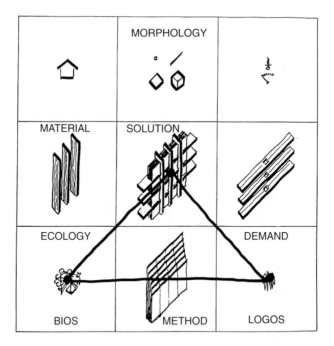

Fig. C1.11 The relation of the basic model and the general building model for joints. In Part C we focus on a selected number of factors, which are arranged in the general building model. Here the outer cells/aspects of the model are incorporated in the three systems of the general building model.

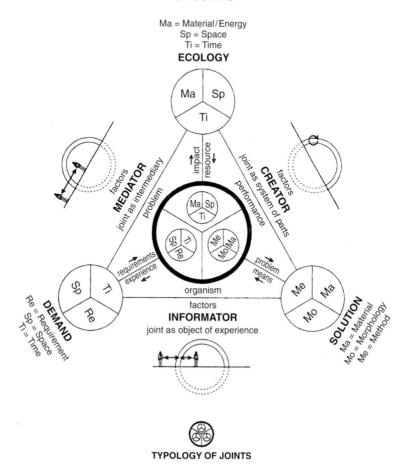

Fig. C1.12   General building model of joints. The joint is specifically seen as a 'solution' deriving from 'demand' within the possibilities of 'ecology'. The joint will be understood as intermediary (1), as system of parts (2), and as object of experience (3). Within the parameters of space and time there are the requirements for demand and material/energy that are relevant for ecology; the solution of material, morphology and method is based on this observation.

Defining the systems

Let us return to the three systems in the general building model: ecology, demand and solution. These are defined in more detail before looking at their relationship to one another.

Ecology (see Fig. C1.13)

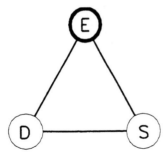

Fig. C1.13   Ecology.

We distinguish the three levels: abiotic, biotic and conceptual. Each level is characterised by matter, space and time properties.

■ Abiotic consists of the four basic elements of fire (light and heat), water, air and earth (meaning only minerals here) in a certain place at a certain time.
■ Biotic consists of the living organisms, in a certain place at a certain time, that depend on the abiotic level for their existence.
■ Conceptual consists of the ideas and artefacts for fulfilling the needs and goals in life in a certain place at a certain time. It is on this level that consciousness and culture manifest themselves. This level depends on the abiotic and biotic levels for its existence.

Demand (see Fig. C1.14)

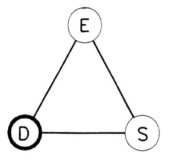

Fig. C1.14   Demand.

We have physiological, physical and psychological requirements in a certain place at a certain time. These requirements
can be met for the most part by the existing ecology (understood
here as environment for ourselves); a varying fraction of these
requirements can be resolved by our inner-self (consciousness
through meditation). But the remaining shortcomings must be
resolved by actively transforming our environment, that is, by
adapting ecology.

Solution (see Fig. C1.15)

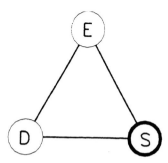

Fig. C1.15   Solution.

One kind of transformation of ecology (and eventually demand)
is brought about by the act of building. Building is concerned
with bringing certain matter, in a certain form, to a certain
place, at a certain time. To narrow it down further we can see
the process as material acquiring a particular morphology by a
particular method.
   Morphology is to be understood here as:

▪ shape (configuration) of parts;
▪ size (dimensions) of parts; and
▪ position (direction/orientation/location) of parts.

Method enhances and enables the change of material and
morphology.

Relationships

Now that we have defined the systems we can look into the
relationships. For each of the three factors there is a specific

set of performance criteria to be achieved by the joint solution. But what are the factors that must be dealt with in a joint? The answer to this question depends on the way in which we look at joints. We can consider our joints from three distinct perspectives, namely the joint as mediator, creator and 'informator' (see below and also Chapter C2). We do this by comparing the relationship of two systems to the third system.

Ecology–demand ↔ solution (see Fig. C1.16)

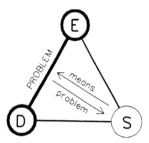

Fig. C1.16   Ecology – demand: solution.

When relating 'ecology' as environment to the requirements of 'demand' we realise there is no absolute fit (causing a problem). We are confronted with too much or too little of certain factors, being:

- light;
- air;
- temperature;
- moisture;
- sound;
- field;
- view;
- minerals;
- plants;
- animals; and
- people.

What we need is a solution acting as an intermediary that controls the passage of these factors. This is why we build in the first place! Here we consider the building and its joints as an intermediary. The solution – the building and its joints – acts as a mediator between the environment and ourselves.

Solution–ecology ↔ demand (see Fig. C1.17)

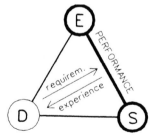

Fig. C1.17 Solution – ecology: demand.

The interaction of 'solution' and 'ecology' results in a performance of the total environment, resulting in the required experiences stated by 'demand'. In this relationship between solution and ecology we deal with the possibilities, probabilities, preferences of how to build (solution) on one hand and maintain the right quality of the environment (ecology) on the other hand. We are talking about the whole life cycle of the building and its joints and its impact on ecology. Factors of that life cycle are:

- execution;
- durability; and
- maintenance/recycling.

Here we consider the building and its joints as a system of parts in its role as a creator.

Demand–solution ↔ ecology (see Fig. C1.18)

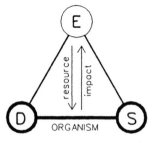

Fig. C1.18 Demand – solution: ecology.

Here we relate demand directly to the building (solution). Together it works as an organism. Ecology serves as a resource to the organism, and the organism has a certain impact on the ecology. Conditional for being an organism is that we know and understand the building as an extension of ourselves. Understanding and appreciating joints is based on experiencing the relationship between the joint as both creator and mediator. How we experience this depends on the following factors:

- material;
- image; and
- control.

We are able to see the relationship between the building as a mediator and the building as a creator. In this sense the building and its joints acts as an object of experience, the 'informator'. (We have deliberately used a new word here; see also Chapter C2.)

Ecology–demand–solution ↔ typology (see Fig. C1.19)

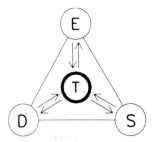

Fig. C1.19   Ecology – demand – solution: typology.

In the middle where the three systems meet we should develop knowledge, that is, the level of integrated knowledge typical for displaying the relationship between the three systems: this knowledge is in the form of a typology. We need a typology because a type can only deal with one kind of attribute, whereas typologies can be used to study variables and transitional situations. 'Transitional situations' implies a process, which is included in the meaning of typology here, where the typology of joints is a procedure for developing principles for the parts and for the whole. Chapter C3 explains how this procedure can be applied.

The factors flower

We can now represent the three ways of looking at joints (as mediator, as creator and as informator) and the corresponding factors in a 'factors flower' with the typological knowledge in the centre (see Fig. C1.20). To comply with each factor it is necessary to apply specific shapes, sizes and positions of parts in the joints. For each distinguished factor these specific shapes, sizes and positions are typical and thereby factor-bound. These typical factor-bound principles of shapes, sizes and positions must be translated or interpreted for each specific joint situation. In the case of a joint between a window-frame and an exterior wall the principles to be considered relating to moisture will be interpreted in a slightly different way compared with a joint between an exterior wall and a roof.

When we compare all the factors, considering their interpretations of the principles of shapes, sizes and positions for one and the same joint situation, then we must distinguish to what

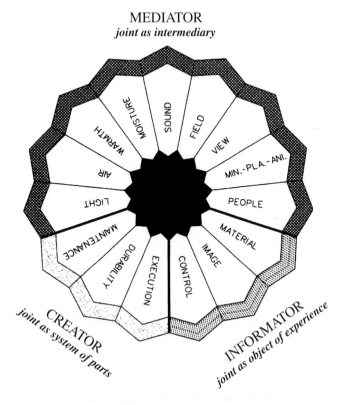

Fig. C1.20 Factors flower.

extent all the shapes, sizes and positions are co-operative with, independent of, or opposing to each other. When relationships are opposing, we must seek to resolve the situation through the application of solution principles in our designs.

Unfortunately, this does not reveal itself too readily. This knowledge must be developed, progressing step by step through a certain procedure, a typical procedure, in order to determine joint solution principles. We refer to both the procedure and the outcome as a typology of joints. Our nine-step development procedure will be explained in Chapter C3. In this procedure the nine-step factor requirements (derived from the three ways of viewing joints, namely as mediator, creator and informator) and solution principles can be traced and judged by the various agents in building. The intention is that all participants should eventually understand the morphological method, essentially a common language of detailing that is analogous to our written language.

C2 THE LANGUAGE OF DETAIL

Every type of construction has its own mode of handling, which must be understood if detailing is to be successful. For example, the detailing of a single-storey building in load-bearing brickwork has different rules to detailing the same building in, say, timber-frame construction. During their career, designers tend to favour certain ways of doing things, and the manner in which they detail buildings often becomes part of their trademark or design signature – detail as a language. Throughout this book we have been discussing and moving towards a typology of joints to support an environmentally friendly approach to construction. In effect it is a language of details and principles that can be applied by designers to realise ecological design. If we are to develop a morphological method of detailing that is understood by all contributors to the design and construction process, then we need to look at a common language: the language of detail.

The language analogy

Through the deconstruction of the detail into its component parts (both its physical and procedural elements) identification of different layers of meaning – a language – will emerge. This process of simplification makes it possible to reconsider detailing from a new perspective, in this case an ecological one, although the process holds true for different perspectives and for different priorities. From a greater understanding of the joint and its morphology we are better equipped to break new ground in our thinking and application of architectural details, that is, we are better equipped to readdress our language of details. We are then in a position to improve the manner in which we build, maintain and disassemble buildings. Once we start to think about the language of detail design we start to question some fundamental issues. For example, to what extent does the language of detail drive the conceptual thinking and conceptual design process? How does the designer's cookbook of standard solutions stand up to such analysis? In grappling with these and associated questions, combined with a better understanding of the language of detail, we are better equipped to address detailing as an art.

There are at least two different ways in which to understand (and to speak) the language of detail. The first is to recognise specific languages of detail as characteristic, (arche)typical manners of how a detail can appear. This appearance will be determined by, among others, the following:

- production process, e.g. workmanlike or mechanical;
- material choice, e.g. hard or soft, warm or cool;
- visual appearance, e.g. shape and form, colour and texture.

Depending on the applied qualifications, as given in the examples above, we recognise that a detail can speak a certain language. A detail expresses in its visual appearance more or less the production process, the chosen materials and maybe some other messages (intended or otherwise), such as intelligence, smartness, complication and simplicity. It might be that details also 'speak' about their embedding within a philosophical and theoretical framework. If we look carefully we can see where details come from, when they came into existence, from which designer or school, and from which tradition or culture they were derived (their place and meaning). Details also show us their function and the goals they serve. It follows that a detail remains a phenomenon in itself (see Fig. C2.1).

The second way to recognise the language of detail is to understand the surprising similarity between architecture and language: a morphological language.

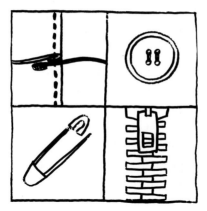

Fig. C2.1(a) Details are essential everywhere. An analogy of preconditional detailing in the art of tailoring.

Fig. C2.1(b) Taped seams showing tailoring techniques used in building.

Morphological language

Again we start with a simple question: Why language? The simple answer is that we need language to enable us to reach our project goals. Where people work together, being the rule, there must be a means of communication. That means a common language that is understood by each person in the communication process. That same language is also the means to develop new ideas, messages and solutions. So, why not a language in building that is analogous to our linguistic language, where 'analogy' is defined as 'resemblance in essentials between things or statements otherwise different'?

The language we develop for detailing buildings must not only be comparable to meet the criteria of analogy, it must also be operational within the world of design and construction, that is, it must be practical. In many respects we already have a common language in building, based on the images we draw of the individual parts, components assemblies and the building whole. So it would be sensible to base our language on morphology, the study of the form of things. What we set out to do was to develop a morphological language, which would then allow us to devise a morphological method for developing solution principles for joints in building.

For example, if we were to state that 'we want to be comfortable' (a requirement of demand) – and we know there is a limit to the type and amount of material we can use for building (relationship between resources of ecology and impact on ecology), and we also know that we must gain and contain heat by the building envelope (solution) – then we have a lot of 'translating' to do before the three systems 'communicate'. Knowing that we will eventually come to the point of determining a solution that is defined in terms of morphology and method, it follows that a morphological language may be a useful tool from which to develop joint solutions. It should be noted that the term 'principle' has been applied several times; likewise within the morphological method we will be developing principles. We can now apply the analogy to the morphological language.

Letters → Alphabet

The 'first principles' of shape are straight, slanted, curved (see Fig. C2.2).

Morphemes

When focusing on certain factors separately, certain combinations of the basic shapes become 'meaningful'. These factor-bound combinations are called *factor principles* (see Fig. C2.3).

ALPHABET

— \ ⌒

BASIC FORMS

Fig. C2.2

MORPHEMES

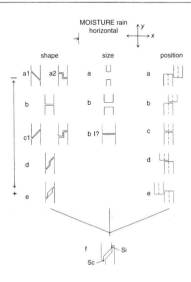

FACTOR PRINCIPLES

Fig. C2.3

WORDS

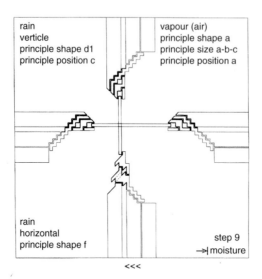

rain	vapour (air)
verticle	principle shape a
principle shape d1	principle size a-b-c
principle position c	principle position a

rain	
horizontal	step 9
principle shape f	→| moisture

<<<

FACTOR TYPOLOGIES

Fig. C2.4

Words → Vocabulary

When we apply these factor principles in the framework of a total specific joint situation, then we can develop *factor typologies* (see Fig. C2.4).

Sentence

When we combine these factor typologies, then we can develop a *general typology* for a specific joint situation. The collection of all joint situations of a building results in a collection or system of general typologies, analogous to a coherent literary entity, being a poem or prose (see Fig. C2.5).

Grammar

The grammar of the morphological method is actually the *rules of composition*. The rules of composition can be divided into two parts:

SENTENCES

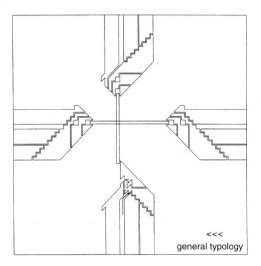

```
<<<
general typology
```

GENERAL TYPOLOGIES

Fig. C2.5

- *The formal rules of the grid:* In order to achieve modularity a grid has been defined including rules for applying the basic shapes of 'straight, slanted, curved' (see Fig. C2.6).
- *The content rules governing performance:* In order to achieve high-level quality of joints, rules must be stated governing the development of factor typologies and general typologies. These rules can be stated in the form of hypotheses, and in recognition of the objective of this research of developing joints, which supports sustainable development, they are called *ecology hypotheses*.

We see that we can extend the analogy between language and morphological method to all the levels distinguished here. Yet there is one essential difference between the two. The sentence is *sequential*: words have specific positions of 'before' and 'after' in relation to each other. In contrast, the general typology is *synchronic*: factor typologies have the same positions for a specific joint situation. It should be noted that at a certain moment not

GRAMMAR

GRID RULES

Fig. C2.6

all factors are 'active'. In the course of time there is a fluctuation of factors being 'active' and 'passive' in varying combinations when considering all factors. This means that the factor typologies also fluctuate according to their status of active or passive. This 'fluctuation' of factors and factor typologies poses one of the most difficult problems to deal with in building.

A typology of joints

We can extend the analogy between language and the morphological method further, when considering the separate categories of factors according to the general building model (GBM) as presented in Chapter C1.

Category A – intermediary

In category A, the joint/detail is seen as a mediator.

In language the sentence is a means of conveying information about an object, situation or event. The specific information results from selection within the whole realm of reality. In the joint there is a comparative process of selection and control of degree of passage. In both cases we are only interested in the actual consequences of the intermediary. In the case of the joint the consequence could be a certain climate inside the building, causing a certain state of wellbeing, possibly triggering certain actions.

In the case of the sentence the consequence could be certain information that causes a certain state of mind or even triggers taking certain actions. In this sense this relationship is stated to be *pragmatic* (from the Greek *pragma*, deed; *prassein*, to act, to do), which evaluates any assertion solely by its practical consequences and its bearing on human interests.

The question here is about the usefulness of the joint in the sense of what it does in the context of the whole and how it is appreciated. What does this mean to the user? For example, when someone says: 'It's nice weather today' we can state the following: Of all the possible topics present in the context of the moment that person selects just one of them, and in addition characterises it. The question we can now pose ourselves is whether the selected topic interests us, and whether we can agree with the other person's judgement. What we can say for sure is that the remark influences our understanding of the context. Analogously the joint could filter out certain sounds coming from the outside, leaving other sounds to reach us on the inside. Did we wish for such a situation? Furthermore, are we satisfied with the limited information?

Category B – experiences

In category B the joint/detail is seen as an informator.

In language the sentence itself has its own quality, which we can appreciate. It is especially the degree of appreciation that is responsible for the distinction we make between 'literature' and ordinary prose. In the case of the joint we also can speak of appreciating the joint itself. In both cases we are interested in the meaning the object has for us, meaning being based on the physical, physiological and spiritual experience. In the case of the joint, meaning and its appreciation concerns the joint in relation to its function within the other two categories:

- Category A: How does the morphology of the joint express what it does considering its function of selecting and controlling the passage of phenomena present in the context?
- Category C: How does the morphology of the joint reveal what the composition is of the joint, the parts of which it is composed and how these parts are assembled?

In the case of the sentence, meaning and its appreciation concerns the sentence in relation to its function within the other two categories:

- Category A: How does the morphology of the sentence express what it does considering its function of selecting and characterising phenomena present in the context?
- Category C: How does the morphology of the sentence reveal the composition of the sentence, the parts of which it is composed and how these parts are assembled?

In this sense this relationship is stated to be *semantic* (from the Greek word *semantikos*, significant), relating to meaning in language.

The question here is about the significance of the joint itself, its meaning and our appreciation. In the example of the statement 'It's nice weather today' we might be of the opinion that this sentence hardly expresses our true experience and feelings about the atmosphere. 'The water drops, trembling on the leaves, glistening in the sun's golden rays during the shower, provide such a refreshing experience after so many weeks of drought…' might express the situation much more appropriately, but for sure we can state that this sentence as such will be appreciated more for its aesthetic quality. It must be noted that it is often difficult to isolate the semantic from the pragmatic qualities. It is the context of the situation that always influences our appreciation of the object itself. The difficulty is only in the sense of analysis of reality: reality reveals itself by synthesised experiences, meaning all three kinds of relationships defining the categories.

Category C – system of parts

In category C the joint/detail is seen as a creator.

In language the sentence is a composition of words according to certain rules of grammar. In the case of joints we have parts composed according to certain rules of composition. In both cases we are interested in the relationship between the parts and the whole. In this sense this relationship is stated to be *syntactic* (from the Greek *syntaxis* – *syn*, together; *tassein*, to put in order) where syntax relates to sentence construction; the grammatical arrangement of words in speech or writing to show their connection and relation; set of rules governing this arrangement.

In the example of the sentence 'It's nice weather today' we can distinguish the various words that have various functions such as subject, verb, adjective, object, adverb, and that are placed in the sequence that complies with the rules of grammar. This takes us on to the issue of style rules for architectural detailing.

Style rules

When writing a message we can choose to keep it short or we can go for an elaborate version. Likewise, we can choose to use difficult words or conversely we can try to keep our language simple and to the point through the use of plain words. In design we have similar choices. We can say it does not matter how many parts we need to form the joint, or we can say the fewer parts needed the better. Considering the shape of parts, we can say we want to keep the shape of distinct parts as simple as possible; conversely the shapes may be as complex as our imagination allows.

The point we are making here is that there are choices to be made. Choices determine further development of joints in particular and the development of the building in general. Remember that the whole is the sum of the parts. These choices must, obviously, be based on certain definite objectives. Let us state that an important objective is to support sustainable development in building. Now in order to get this operational we can state certain rules. Application of these rules should, to a great extent, guide the process of design towards our goal of sustainable development. These style rules, called ecology hypotheses, are based on the individual categories of mediator, creator and informator (see Fig. C2.7). The belief is that if these style rules are applied it will lead to ecological as well as economical solutions in detail design.

Application of style rules must be seen as a design aid that guides development of shape, size and position of the parts and the whole in a joint. In that sense design is a very concrete thing. Unfortunately, words alone won't help; we must develop by using the right kind of language, and that is in shapes, sizes and positions. Two morphological principles are presented and compared below, considering their performances in all three categories.

STYLE RULES

Ecology-Hypothesis A1: (category A: the joint as intermediary)
When the performance of the joint (meeting-fixing-sealing) is such that the requirements of Demand are met with a minimal need for additional energy/ matter, then building in general complies more with sustainable development.

Ecology-Hypothesis B1: (category B: the joint as object of experience)
When the experience of the joint is such that we acquire a better understanding of the principles of morphology in relation to the 'forces' of Ecology, then building in general complies more with sustainable development.

Ecology-Hypothesis C1: (factor Execution of category C: joint as system of parts)
When the morphology of only the main building components ensures the required performances of 'meeting', 'fixing' and 'sealing' in the joint, then building in general complies more with sustainable development.

Ecology-Hypothesis C2: (factor Durability of category C: joint as system of parts)
When the performances of 'meeting', 'fixing' and 'sealing' ensure an optimal durability of the parts in the joint, then building in general complies more with sustainable development.

Ecology-Hypothesis C3: (factor Maintenance of category C: joint as system of parts)
When the performances of 'meeting', 'fixing' and 'sealing' comply with assembly and disassembly sequences in relation to expected (Durability) or desired lifetimes of parts, then building in general complies more with sustainable development.

ECOLOGY HYPOTHESES

Fig. C2.7

Comparison between two morphological principles

When we have an exterior wall there are in general two principles for preventing the passage of water from the exterior to the interior. Figure C2.8 illustrates the single-plane principle and Fig. C2.9 the fish-scale principle.

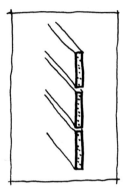

Fig. C2.8

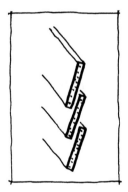

Fig. C2.9

The joint as intermediary (mediator) (A)

First of all we must make the distinction between a one-stage sealing and a two-stage sealing. In the case of a two-stage sealing there is a 'back-up' provision for preventing passage of water all the way to the interior. In the case of the single-plane principle it is allowable that water leaks through the horizontal seams. In the case of the fish-scale principle, leaks are also possible due to air pressures and capillary forces. In the case of a one-stage sealing process the single-plane principle offers a bigger problem than the fish-scale principle. If water was to leak through to the interior, then extra ventilation and heat would be required to get rid of the excessive moisture, but this would not accord with the ecology hypothesis A1:

> When the performance of the joint (meeting, fixing, sealing) is such that the requirements of 'demand' are met without the need for additional energy, then the building in general complies more with sustainable development.

Improvements must therefore be made in order to achieve the required performance. For that we must look at the joint as a system of parts.

The joint as system of parts (creator) (C)

In the single-plane principle we could add an extra jointing part such as a sealant or aluminium Z-profile, but this would not agree with ecology hypothesis C1 considering the factor 'execution':

> When the morphology of only the main building components ensures the required performances of 'meeting', 'fixing' and 'sealing', then the building in general complies more with sustainable development.

So what we do is adapt the shape of the main components such as proposed in Fig. C2.10.

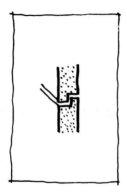

Fig. C2.10

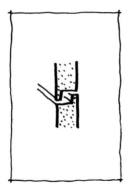

Fig. C2.11

Sealing against water can be furthermore improved by applying a so-called relief cavity in the joint face, as illustrated in Fig. C2.11.

The fish-scale principle is on the whole actually an improvement on the single-plane principle due to adapting the position of the components. In Fig. C2.12 we see a hybrid solution, having the fish-scale principle on the outside (where you really need it) and the single-plane principle on the inside. This is the well-known bevel-siding (bevel edge) solution.

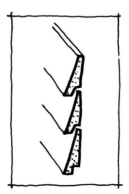

Fig. C2.12

Performance of the fish-scale principle can be improved likewise by applying the relief cavity as shown in Fig. C2.13.

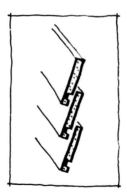

Fig. C2.13

Another important factor to consider is the durability of the parts in the joint, ecology hypothesis C2:

> When the performances of 'meeting', 'fixing' and 'sealing' ensure an optimal durability of the parts in the joint, then the building in general complies more with sustainable development.

In the case of the single-plane principle it is obvious that the top of the components on the outside is very vulnerable to decay due to the forces of sunlight and water.

The third and last factor to consider in this category is maintenance, ecology hypothesis C3:

> When the performance of 'meeting', 'fixing' and 'sealing' comply with assembly and disassembly sequences in relation to expected (durability) or desired lifetimes of parts, then the building in general complies more with sustainable development.

If the fixing components are accessible (e.g. screws), then it is possible in both principles to assemble or disassemble an individual part without causing unnecessary damage.

The joint as object of experience (informator) (B)

Ecology hypothesis B1:

> When the experience of the joint is such that we acquire a better understanding of the principles of morphology in

relation to the 'forces' of ecology, then the building in general complies more with sustainable development.

The question here is whether we experience the relationship between the joint as intermediary and the joint as system of parts, or, to put it in plain English: Do we understand why the joint looks like it does? Do we, or are we able to, 'read' what the joint is doing? Do we have the intellectual skills and practical knowledge to do so as and when necessary?

Knowledge and understanding of our environment supports our feeling of care and concern. Ignorance leads to indifference and this may be the greatest danger for an ecologically sustainable world. In the single-plane principle the morphology in Fig. C2.11 cannot be experienced visually, it is a 'blind' solution. The visual seam itself consists of two lines with a particular spacing. In the fish-scale principle in Fig. C2.13 we can experience the water-shedding performance of the joints; you cannot turn the principle upside down, because then it will no longer work as intended. Only the relief cavity is a 'blind' solution. The principle presents a one-line image, therefore posing no problem of dimensional deviations as in the two-line image of the single-plane principle. Do not underestimate the cost of getting the seams visually correct! Our conclusion from this brief analysis of two principles is that the fish-scale principle is the better principle for supporting sustainable development in building.

Consequences

Once we have concluded that the fish-scale principle is the optimal principle for shedding water, we could ask ourselves what this means for all the joints in the building's exterior surface. If we were to develop a whole building consistently based on this principle, then the whole building environment would present startling new images. But these images would support, in our view, a deeper understanding of the 'diagram of forces' as proposed by Christopher Alexander in his seminal work *Notes on the Synthesis of Form* (1964). Things start to take on more meaning for us; therefore the environment is 'richer' and more satisfying and may result in a greater appreciation of our milieu. As noted earlier, design is about making choices based on compromise and the determination to see a vision through. To do this we need the guiding mechanism of style rules, thus helping to avoid superficial solutions (Figs C2.14 and C2.15).

Fig. C2.14   A building supported by structural columns?

Fig. C2.15   Perhaps not! Some details are for decoration only.

C3 THE NINE-PLUS-ONE STEP PROCEDURE

If we are to design and use more sustainable details we need to reconsider and challenge the tried and tested solutions that are applied in practice with little thought for their impact on the environment. In this chapter we present a nine-step developmental procedure as a tool to develop more sustainable details. A standard joint situation is chosen and optimised according to a nine-step development procedure based on the typology of joints. Once this is complete it is then possible to add materials to our proposed solution, the plus-one step.

A morphological method

In building we reason, develop and communicate by using images, the morphological language. This means we will be applying an alphabet, syllables, morphemes, words and sentences, thereby abiding by the rules of grammar and on the whole expressing a certain style. The alphabet, syllables and morphemes have been developed for this morphological language, along with the rules of grammar and style rules. What we would like to develop further are the words, the vocabulary of detailing. A word in the morphological language is called a 'factor typology'. A factor typology concerns a specific joint situation and a specific factor in which the optimal factor principle (morpheme) is applied. The nine-step procedure provides a systematic approach to the development of new joint solutions, and is applicable to both designers and manufacturers. As such it has implications for new product development and innovative joint solutions.

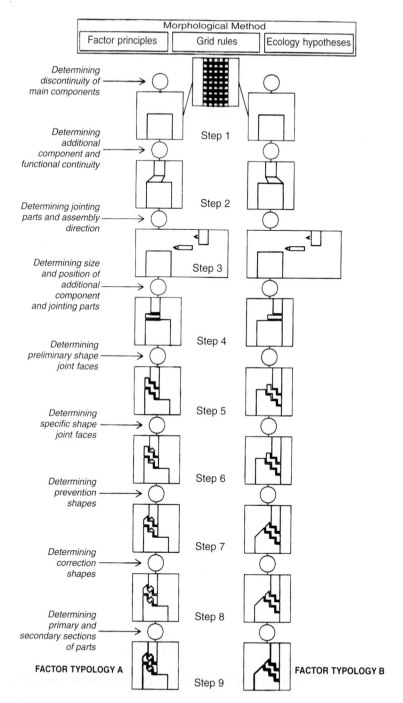

Fig. C3.1   A morphological method for developing factor typologies.

Here we present a procedure to develop a factor typology for joint solutions in nine steps, as illustrated in Fig. C3.1. Each step seeks to manipulate and enhance the joint configuration, resulting in a gradual transformation of the joint morphology. Worked examples of our methodology are shown below; however the steps can be explained as a series of general principles without referring to a specific joint situation.

Step 1: Determine the discontinuity of main components

Present the main components and determine their discontinuity.

Step 2: Determine the functional continuity and additional components required

Determine which part (considering size and position) of the main components should be functionally continuous and link this with the (possible) additional component. The size of the additional component might already be determined, but not its position.

Step 3: Determine the joining (jointing) parts and their assembly direction

Determine the jointing parts to be applied between the main components and the possible additional component. Then determine from which direction assembly and disassembly of possible additional component and jointing parts will take place. There may be more than one possibility to choose from.

Step 4: Determine the size and position of any additional components and the jointing parts

Determine the size and position of additional component and jointing parts relative to each other, and to the main components.

Step 5: Determine the preliminary shape of the joint faces

Apply standard sealing shape for all joint faces. The standard sealing shape has been determined to be air principle C (labyrinth). When we review all factor principles, we see that the 'labyrinth principle' is the most basic principle for sealing: 'air' is the carrier for 'moisture', 'warmth', 'sound', 'minerals' (dust), 'plants' (pollen) and 'animals' (flies). The intention here is to first generalise and then to specify according to specific factor requirements in the steps that follow.

Step 6: Determine the specific shape of the joint faces

A factor might require specific shapes of joint faces in relation to the performance of 'sealing'.

Step 7: Determine the prevention shapes

Prevention shapes are intended to keep the 'load' on the seams as minimal as possible. Examples are shapes of parts resulting in aerodynamic surfaces around seams (air), and the overlap principle for protecting the seams from rain (moisture) penetration.

Step 8: Determine the correction shapes

Correction shapes are to be applied in the joint faces if the measures in the previous steps would not suffice when we consider performance requirements relating to sealing.

Step 9: Determine the primary and secondary sections of the parts

Primary sections of parts are those sections that are essential for an optimal performance considering the specific factor.

Secondary sections could change without actually affecting the optimal performance of the joint. Secondary sections therefore allow solution space for variants. Bold lines represent primary sections.

Summary

As stated earlier, the intention of this nine-step procedure is to develop factor typologies (the words). General typologies (the sentences) are integrated factor typologies applied to a specific joint situation. All the factor typologies can be seen as layers that can be combined to one general typology for one specific joint situation, as shown in Fig. C3.2.

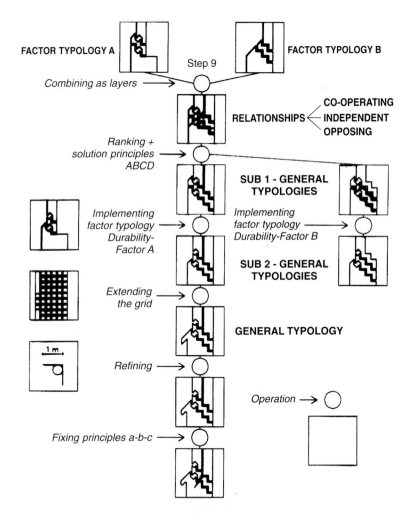

DEVELOPMENT
of
A TYPOLOGY OF JOINTS
supporting sustainable development in building

Fig. C3.2   Development of a typology of joints.

When combining several factor typologies as transparent layers it will become apparent whether relationships are co-operative, independent or opposing. In the case of opposing relationships we will need to rank the most dominant factors and then address them with the intention of making the relationship more harmonious. Then the relationship to the factor 'durability' must be investigated with the intention of further improving the performance. Once this has been done we need to 'refine' the shapes on the level of the module grid. Finally, we can taker a closer look at the application of 'fixing principles' if necessary.

In the three worked examples presented here, a kind of consensus procedure is followed. For a specific joint situation an optimisation procedure is applied by following the same nine steps for a single factor typology, but dealing with a number of factors simultaneously. This method must be seen as a quick scanning method in order to get the full essence of the principle.

Worked example 1: window in a cavity wall

The first example we will use is not just an example of joints, but *the* example of joints in which all possible factors play a role. The case of the window in a cavity wall is, in many respects, concerned with the detailing of a void in the solid, the 'hole in a cavity wall'.

Step 1: Determining discontinuity of main components (mediator/creator)

Here we see the main components of the cavity wall:

- the inner leaf;
- the insulation within the cavity; and
- the outer leaf.

First of all it is very important to know the reasons for this specific 'layering' and the choice of the selected materials and the required dimensions. These will be coloured by a whole range of functional requirements for the wall, e.g. strength, stability, thermal insulation, sound insulation, fire resistance, aesthetics, durability, and so on.

These components (inner and outer walls and insulation) are opaque, thereby prohibiting the passage of 'light' and 'view'. So we need to make a hole, which causes the discontinuity of these main components. Discontinuity means by definition the existence of joints. The size of the opening corresponds with the required quality and quantity of light and view (mediator) (see Fig. C3.3). Please note that the plan and section overlap in all of these steps.

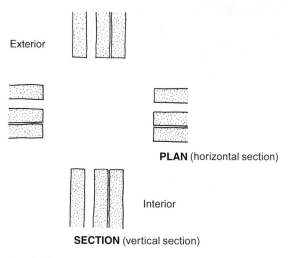

Fig. C3.3

Step 2: Determining the additional component(s) (creator) and functional continuity (mediator)

Considering the passage of air, warmth, moisture, sound, field, minerals, plants, animals and people, there must be functional continuity in the whole wall.

Considering the passage of light and view, this does not have to be continuous, thus the 'hole' in the wall. To meet the requirements of light and view in combination with all other factors we need additional components that must be transparent, i.e. glass (being the state of the art at the moment). We choose to apply two additional glass components, one corresponding with the inner leaf and one with the outer leaf (the reason for this will soon become apparent) (see Fig. C3.4).

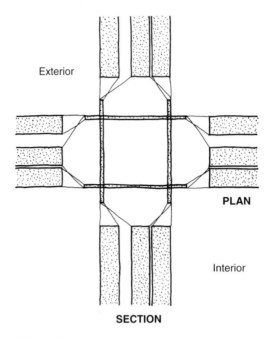

Exterior

PLAN

Interior

SECTION

Fig. C3.4

Step 3: Determining jointing parts and assembly direction (creator)

We have two additional glass components. For the joint between the outer glass component and the outer leaf we determine that there will be a jointing part.

We could have chosen not to apply an additional jointing part. But experience tells us that the performance of 'meeting' (execution), 'fixing' (execution) and 'sealing' (air, also as a carrier of warmth, sound, minerals, plants, animals) cannot be optimal without a mediating jointing part.

We assume here that the additional glass components have the quality of structural (double) glazing, therefore not requiring a window-frame. The outer glass component and its jointing parts will be assembled from the outside. The inner glass component and its jointing parts will be assembled from the inside (see Fig. C3.5).

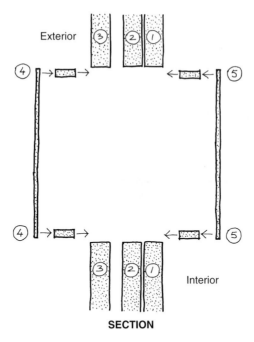

SECTION

Fig. C3.5

Step 4: Determining size and position of possible additional component(s) and jointing parts (creator/ mediator)

The position of the outer glass component will be in the same plane as the exterior of the main outer leaf component. This is because of the optimal performance of 'sealing' considering the factor 'moisture' that will be explained in Step 6.

The position of the inner glass component will be in the same plane as the interior side of the inner leaf. The reason for this considers the factors 'sound' and 'warmth' in relation to the distance between the outer and inner glass components.

The positions of the jointing parts more or less coincide with the glass components.

The sizes of the jointing parts are kept to a minimum and are related to an optimal performance of 'meeting', 'fixing' and 'sealing'. In this step we assume a size that will be tested in the remaining steps, especially the points of 'overlap' in the drawing, which are concerned with the performance of 'sealing' considering the factor 'air' (see Step 5). Note that the size of the transparent opening corresponds with the preferred size in Step 1 (see Fig. C3.6).

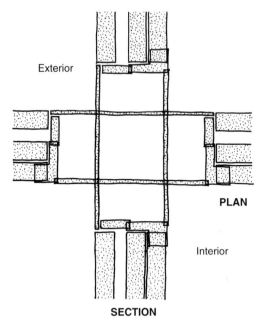

Exterior

PLAN

Interior

SECTION

Fig. C3.6

Step 5: Determining preliminary shape joint faces (mediator)

In Step 4 we have determined the position and size of all distinguished parts. Now we will start shaping these parts, especially where these parts meet each other: the joint faces.

The preliminary shape has been determined to be the optimal 'sealing' shape for the factor 'air', being the 'labyrinth' shape (air principle shape C). When we review all factor principles, we see that the 'labyrinth principle' is the most common principle for sealing. The intention, therefore, is to first generalise in this step and then to specify according to specific factor requirements in the following steps. Note that there is, as yet, no difference between the head, jamb and sill joints (see Fig. C3.7).

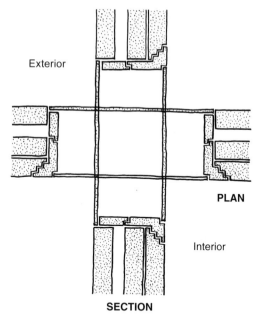

Fig. C3.7

Step 6: Determining specific shape joint faces (mediator)

This step deals with the factors of the mediator only. (Factors of the creator will be dealt with in Step 8 and the factors of the informator in Step 9.)

On the outside we must prevent the passage of moisture. This is the basic performance requirement. One of the most specific principles in order to achieve this is the application of a 'relief cavity' that causes an air pressure drop and also prohibits capillary action. Therefore, there is no passage of moisture further into the wall. We see this where the main outer leaf component, the additional glass component and the jointing part meet each other in the jamb joint. In the head and sill joint it is only the jointing part meeting the glass component.

In the head joint it is essential that the joint faces of the outer leaf and the jointing part are slanted down towards the outside (gravity). A masonry outer leaf may become saturated, thus making the inside surface wet also, so moisture dripping down must be led to the outside. This slanted shape also works for the sill joint and is enforced here with an extra overlapping principle to keep moisture out of the wall. The intention is to keep the insulation layer dry at all times (see Fig. C3.8).

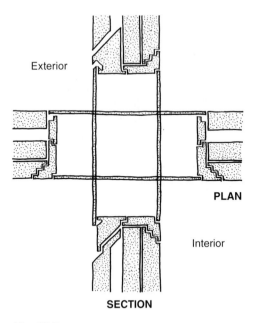

Fig. C3.8

Step 7: Determining prevention shapes (mediator)

Prevention shapes are intended to keep the 'load' on seams to a minimum. Parts joining on the exterior should always be in the same plane at the seam. This is basic in order to prohibit the build up of air pressure in the seam and/or the entrance of moisture. Yet we can protect the seam even more if the outer leaf protrudes, but in such a manner that on the side of the seam the wind is not blocked, but on the other side the protrusion acts as a wind barrier. We see this principle at the jamb joints. At the head joint the protrusion of the outer leaf and of the window-frame protects the seam from moisture (gravity).

At the sill the protrusion of the outer leaf protects the wall under it from moisture and minerals (dirt). The seam between glass and window-frame complies more now to the principle of 'equal planes' (see Fig. C3.9).

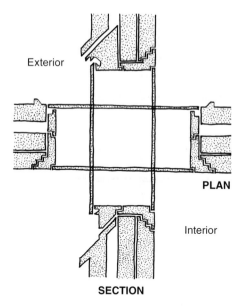

Fig. C3.9

Step 8: Determining correction shapes (creator)

In this step we will investigate whether there are reasons for adjusting shapes because of performance requirements called for by the factors 'execution', 'durability' and 'maintenance', being factors of the category 'creator'.

In the sill joint we must adapt the shape of the joint between interior and exterior window-frame in order to make it possible to assemble the exterior window-frame (execution), after assembly of the interior window-frame (and disassembly of exterior window-frame when the interior window-frame is in position). Furthermore we must extend the glass component in order to protect the (wooden) sill (durability, maintenance). Because of the protrusions of the outer leaf it might be wise to manufacture specific profile parts (execution) (see Fig. C3.10).

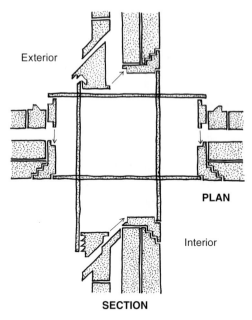

SECTION

Fig. C3.10

Step 9: Determining primary and secondary sections of parts (informator)

In this step we will evaluate the consequences for the factors 'material', 'image' and 'control', being the factors of the category 'informator'.

Everything we have determined so far considering the position, size and shape of parts and whole is based on our present knowledge of the joint seen as mediator and the joint seen as creator. As a result the joint should inform us of this when we experience the joint as mediator and as creator. In this sense 'form follows function'.

For the actual building substance this should be the case for the primary sections, being those sections that are essential for an optimal performance. Secondary sections allow more freedom, especially of shape. Symbols, ornament and reference may be examples of factors that could influence the shape of secondary sections. With symbols, ornaments, reference it is possible to express personal, group, cultural convictions, ideologies, thereby giving identification to buildings, living environments (see Figs C3.11a and C3.11b).

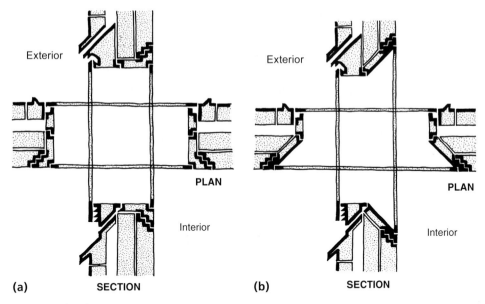

Fig. C3.11(a,b)

Reflection on the process so far

Having gone through the nine-step development process, it is important that we stop to reflect on what we have done and, equally important, what we have not done.

What have we done?

In the nine-step development procedure we have related the performances of 'meeting', 'fixing' and 'sealing' to the three functions of the joint as mediator (pragmatics), creator (syntactics) and informator (semantics). The development is that of a morphological nature, meaning the position, size and shape of parts and whole. The end result in Step 9 is that of a solution principle.

What have we not done?

We have not actually dealt with the specific material characteristics of the parts, for example, wood, stone, brick or glass, or their physical dimensions. Furthermore, the dimensional tolerances that allow easy assembly have not been specified (all drawings comply to the 'grid'). If we are to deal with these aspects, then we must make further choices considering materials and dimensions, and we speak of developing one of the many possible solution variants. So from one solution principle (the abstract) we are able to develop a number of solution variants (the concrete). For this we need an additional step.

Step 9 + 1: Determining a solution variant

Here we will choose materials for all the components identified in the nine-step procedure. In doing so we determine specific behaviour in relation to expansion, contraction and deformation of material due to warmth, moisture, light, air, sound, field, minerals, plants, animals, people and gravity, which causes dimensional deviations. We must, therefore, define tolerances in order to achieve optimal performances in all three categories of creator, mediator and informator.

The following materials/products are chosen for the main components:

- inner leaf – sand-limestone blocks;
- outer leaf – clay bricks;
- insulation – fibreglass.

The following materials/products are chosen for the additional components:

- safety glass.

The following materials/components are chosen for the jointing parts:

- sand-limestone blocks;
- clay bricks;
- timber window-frame.

The joints could now resemble something similar to that illustrated in Figs. C3.12a and C3.12b. Alternatively the 3D illustrations (Fig. C3.12c) represent a different solution (due to different choices when going through the same steps).

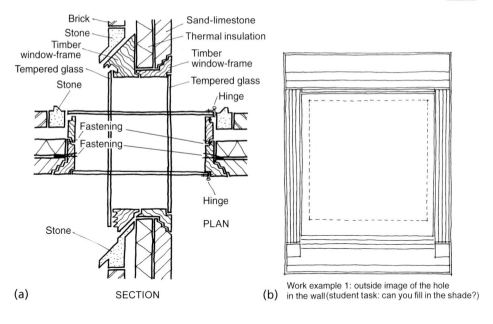

(a)   SECTION

(b) Work example 1: outside image of the hole in the wall (student task: can you fill in the shade?)

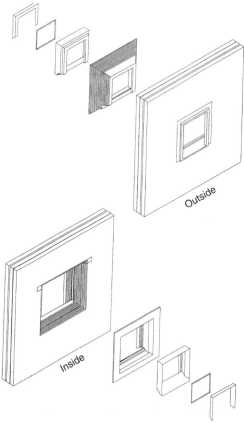

(c)

Fig. C3.12 (a) Window sections. (b) Window elevation. (c) The 3D illustrations represent alternative window frame joints to (a) and (b)

Worked example 2: wall/pitched roof junction

Continuing with our progressive method we offer two further examples to help illustrate the principle further. Worked example 2 continues with the cavity wall, only this time we address the junction between a floor and a pitched roof.

Step 1: Determining the discontinuity of main components (mediator/creator)

The main components are illustrated in Fig. C3.13, namely:

- inner leaf;
- insulation in the cavity;
- outer leaf;
- floor;
- roof (with integral insulation);
- water-shedding layer.

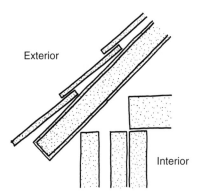

Fig. C3.13

Step 2: Determining the additional component(s) (creator) and functional continuity (mediator)

Functional continuity applies to all factors of 'mediator', so there is no need for additional components to solve functional discontinuity, as illustrated in Fig. C3.14.

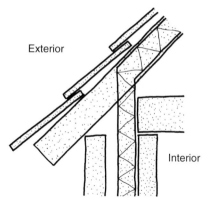

Exterior

Interior

Fig. C3.14

Step 3: Determining jointing parts and assembly direction and sequence (creator). Step 4: Determining size and position of possible additional component(s) and jointing parts (creator/mediator)

A jointing part (no. 3, Fig. C3.15) between the floor and roof components is chosen. Considering all possible sequences of assembly, we would like to finish the roof as soon as possible in order to have a dry building. To be able to erect the outer leaf later we must add the roof overhang afterwards, meaning introducing an additional component (no. 8) for reasons of the factor 'execution' (creator). (Additional components for reasons of factors of 'mediator' are decided in Step 2.).

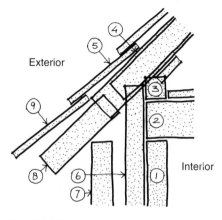

Exterior

Interior

Fig. C3.15

Step 5: Determining preliminary shape joint faces (mediator)

The basic labyrinth principle is applied for the meeting between the additional component and the roof component, between the jointing part and the roof component, and between the water-shedding components and the roof component (see Fig. C3.16a). It is possible to imagine the same principle applied between the floor and the inner leaf, and between the floor and the roof (see Fig. C3.16b).

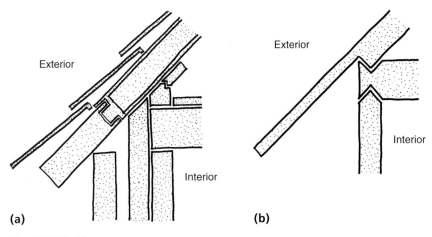

(a)   (b)

Fig. C3.16(a,b)

Step 6: Determining specific shape joint faces (mediator)

Considering the factor 'moisture', the principle of the relief cavity is applied in the joint between the water-shedding components (see Fig. C3.17).

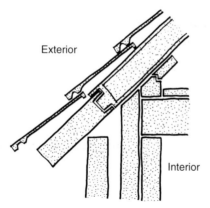

Fig. C3.17

Step 7: Determining prevention shapes (mediator)

There are no specific prevention shapes to be applied.

Step 8: Determining correction shapes (creator)

Execution: In order to accommodate varying angles in the joint between the floor and the roof, the basic form of the circle is applied in the jointing part.

Durability/maintenance: The size of the additional component is minimised in order to maximise durability and minimise maintenance. A gutter further increases the protection to the wall (see Fig. C3.18).

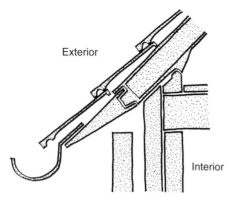

Fig. C3.18

Step 9: Determining primary and secondary sections of parts (informator)

The shedding of water, the collection of water, the protection of the wall, the outer leaf being a non-loadbearing skin, well ventilated – this we can see and understand: The joint informs us of the relationship between the mediator and the creator. The essential sections to achieve this are called the primary sections and are illustrated in Fig. C3.19.

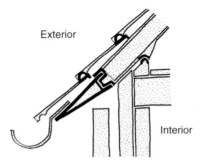

Exterior

Interior

Fig. C3.19

Step 9 + 1: Determining a solution variant

Here we will choose specific materials for all components, thereby having specific behaviour considering expansion, contraction and deformation due to warmth, moisture, light, air, sound, field, minerals, plants, animals, people and gravity, causing dimensional deviations. We must therefore define tolerances in order to achieve optimal performances in all three categories of creator, mediator and informator.

The following materials/products are chosen for the main components:

- inner leaf: sand-limestone blocks;
- insulation: fibreglass (or better, an organic material);
- outer leaf: bricks;
- floor: prefabricated concrete (or better, timber joists);
- roof: stressed wooden skin panels;
- water-shedding components: roof tiles.

The following materials/products are chosen for the additional component:

- roof overhang: timber (wood).

The following materials/products are chosen for the jointing parts:

- roof plate: wood and steel.

The joint could now look like Fig. C3.20.

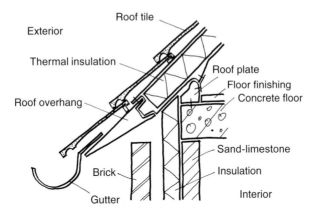

Fig. C3.20

Worked example 3: wall/flat roof junction

Our third and final example continues with the theme of the cavity wall; however, instead of a pitched roof now we address the junction of the wall with a flat roof.

Step 1: Determining the discontinuity of main components (mediator/creator)

The main components are illustrated in Fig. C3.21, namely:

- inner leaf;
- insulation in the cavity;
- outer leaf;
- roof;
- insulation on top;
- watertight membrane.

Exterior

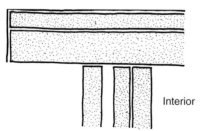

Interior

Fig. C3.21

Step 2: Determining the additional component(s) (creator) and functional continuity (mediator)

Functional continuity applies to all factors of 'mediator', but knowing beforehand that the roof will be of prefabricated concrete components, we choose to apply an additional component for the overhang in order to simplify the solution for a continuous insulation layer (warmth), without needing to go around the overhang (see Fig. C3.22). Wishing to apply a loose watertight membrane we will need weight on top (see Fig. C3.22a).

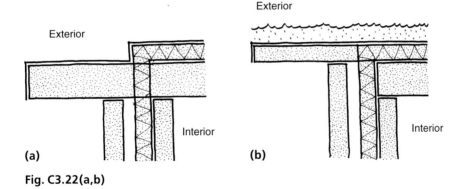

Exterior

Exterior

Interior

Interior

(a)

(b)

Fig. C3.22(a,b)

Step 3: Determining jointing parts and assembly direction and sequence (creator). Step 4: Determining size and position of possible additional component(s) and jointing parts (creator/mediator). Step 5: Determining preliminary shape joint faces (mediator)

Here again we decide on a quick erection of the roof and afterwards apply the wall insulation and the outer leaf, with the advantage of keeping the cavity fairly dry. The additional component for the overhang is increased in height in order to be able to hold the weight layer on the membrane (see Fig. C3.23).

Exterior

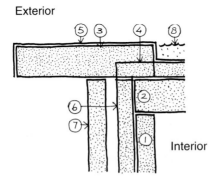

Interior

Fig. C3.23

Step 6: Determining specific shape joint faces (mediator)

Considering the factor moisture, the upper side of the overhang is slanted in order to guide water away from the potentially vulnerable joint. A special metal profile is used here to finish the membrane (factor moisture).

The additional component is finished on the front side and underneath in order to prevent the ingress of birds and mice (animals). The dotted lines suggest an alternative position for this finish (see Fig. C3.24).

Exterior

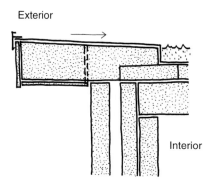

Interior

Fig. C3.24

Step 7: Determining prevention shapes (mediator)

No specific prevention shapes are applied.

Step 8: Determining correction shapes (creator)

Durability/maintenance: The shape of the additional overhang component is adjusted in order to minimise exposure to sun and rain, thereby extending its durability and minimising maintenance (see Fig. C3.25).

Exterior

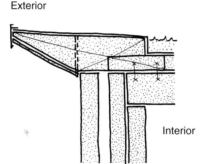

Interior

Fig. C3.25

Step 9: Determining primary and secondary sections of parts (informator)

The shedding of water, the collection of water, the protection of the wall, the outer leaf being a non-loadbearing skin, well ventilated, etc. – this we can see and understand. The joint informs us of the relationship between the mediator and the creator. The essential sections to achieve this are called the primary sections and are illustrated in Fig. C3.26.

Exterior

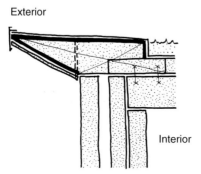

Interior

Fig. C3.26

Step 9 + 1: Determining a solution variant

Here we will choose specific materials for all components, thereby having specific behaviour considering expansion, contraction and deformation due to warmth, moisture, light, air, sound, field, minerals, plants, animals, people and gravity, causing dimensional deviations. We must therefore define tolerances in order to achieve optimal performances in all three categories of creator, mediator and informator.

The following materials/products are chosen for the main components:

- inner leaf: sand-limestone blocks;
- insulation: fibreglass;
- outer leaf: bricks;
- roof: prefabricated concrete.

The following materials/products are chosen for the additional components:

- roof overhang: wood;
- roof built-up weight: vegetation.

The following materials/products are chosen for the jointing part:

- roof edge: metal profile.

The joint could now look like that illustrated in Fig. C3.27.

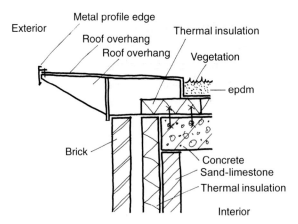

Fig. C3.27

Reflection

The nine-plus-one step procedure is a way of developing details that comply with a more environmentally friendly approach to building. When developing a detail for a joint situation the designer will go through the procedure several times (design being an iterative process) with several agents (e.g. client, users, architect, technologist, various engineers, manufacturers, contractor, sociologist, psychologist, facilities manager, medical/health experts, ecologists, and so on). After a while it is rewarding to take the same joint situation and go through the steps again. Things may have changed (knowledge, people, technologies), most likely leading to a different outcome. Likewise, if we take the same joint situation but address it in a different place in the world, the outcome is likely to be different (due to different climate, culture and so on).

We have shown three worked examples, of which the first is the most complex, considering the number of factors involved. We have deliberately gone from the most complex to the more simple. In doing so we have shortened the steps in order to show how a designer may approach the procedure in practice. Our intention is to give an idea of how the procedure works, rather than to go into too much depth. It should be noted that more development work has yet to be done on the procedure and the details of all possible joint situations.

When we look at the performance of the joint it must be noted that development of the joints in this nine-plus-one procedure is especially focused on the performance of sealing, being directly linked to the performance of meeting. The performance of fixing tends to lead to solutions that are more independent, such as hinges, in contrast to the continuous character of sealing within the overall joint system.

C4 MANAGING THE DETAILING PHASE

Throughout this book we have emphasised the importance of the detail. We have highlighted the interrelationships between conceptual design of the whole building, the details and construction as paramount to creative detailing. We have been primarily concerned with building technologies and their correct application within an environmentally responsible framework. Now we need to consider an equally important and necessary issue, the management of the detailing process. This is an area that naturally falls within the design management field and which also has an overlap with the fields of production and construction management. The purpose of this chapter is to look at the management of the detailing process, mainly from the perspective of the designer while also recognising the importance of collaboration with others. Experience shows us that a lot of effort expended on the development and refinement of the details could be wasted if the management of the process, that is, the communication of design intent, is handled poorly.

An argument for effective management

Take a moment to think about the world's finest wines, gourmet foods, and so on. They have four common factors. First is the use of the finest material, second is the use of the best craftsmen and third is attention to detail – factors also common to the world's best buildings and addressed earlier in this book. The fourth factor is not quite so obvious – the professional management of the entire process, from the sourcing of materials and craftsmen, through attention to detail at all stages of development to the marketing and presentation of the completed product and subsequent feedback, all within a quality framework. Good management is rarely noticed (we could argue that it is deliberately invisible); unfortunately it is when things are poorly managed and problems arise that people take note because it affects them in an adverse way.

Design and construction projects involve a large number of different people and organisations, each with differing aims and objectives. It is important, therefore, to recognise that the quality of the detail will not be at the top of everyone's list of priorities. For example, continual pressure to reduce costs and save time can lead to pressure to revise or change details. Such changes can be made hastily and with insufficient consideration for the long-term durability of the constructed works. While we put forward a case for holistic participation throughout design and construction, we recognise that many projects may not aspire to such altruistic aims. To develop and deliver more sustainable details and buildings requires the professional management of both the design office and the individual projects that form the lifeblood of the organisation. Architectural design management literature is concerned with implementing mechanisms to facilitate the transfer of design intent. Design management is primarily concerned with managing people and information within set time frames and with known resources. The competence of the people assigned to the task and the quality of the information produced and subsequently transferred through formal and informal communication routes is critical to realising quality and value.

As noted earlier, details are developed for a particular project at a particular time, that is, they have a place and meaning. The process through which they are developed – a phase we know as detail design, materialisation or architectural engineering – is coloured by factors specific to that particular project. Client requirements, physical site conditions, planning, building regulations and codes, input of consultants and user groups are just a few of the factors that make each project, and hence its details, unique. The process is important as a vehicle to deliver a quality product and our ultimate focus must be on the product. Once the building is complete the process is quickly forgotten, but the building remains for a very long time. This process can never be perfect because people are involved, and we are, by nature, unpredictable. So the best we can do is design, implement and monitor managerial systems that help the detailer in his or her daily endeavours, systems that provide support but which also allow and encourage creativity.

This takes us into the area of architectural design management, the synergistic management of individual projects and the organisation(s) in which they are designed and detailed. Designers' core values are concerned with creative thinking and research; the challenge for design managers is to create and maintain an environment in which this activity can take place effectively and efficiently. It follows that the manner in which individual projects are programmed, that is, the time allocated to specific stages of the project, is critical. We cannot expect consistency while people are constantly under considerable pressure to deliver within very short time frames.

We have put forward an argument for concentrating on a more responsible approach to detailing and construction. It should be clear that it is fundamental that conceptual design must deal with both the level of the whole building and the level of the detail. Here, we need to reiterate the environmental argument, because without adequate managerial control there is a real danger that considerable effort expended on detailing can be compromised, or in the worst case lost, as the project progresses through to completion. We strongly believe that the control of the details should remain within the remit of the designers and engineers; however, some contractual arrangements prevent this, with decisions made by others with different agendas. Changes to the details, whether deliberate or accidental, will affect the performance of the building and will affect the environmental impact of the building (some for better, some for worse). Therefore it is important to be aware of design control and the implications of design changes from the outset if we are to achieve quality buildings that demonstrate good value for our clients and have a positive impact on our environment (see Fig. C4.1).

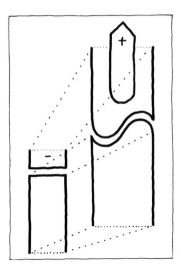

Fig. C4.1 We extend the conceptual area into detailing and production. The new focus in terms of space has not only to be on the detail beside the 'great shape' but also – in terms of time – on a preparatory period and on an optimal relation between durability and sustainability. All these new dimensions need a paramount place in designing conceptually.

Design control

Designers know – or find out very quickly – that the development of a building design may well appear linear and progressive but is in fact iterative. The process is circular, cross-referential and involves a certain amount of backtracking as the designer attempts to avoid non-productive routes to achieve his or her goal. The majority of designers also work on more than one project at any one time, thus the working day may be fragmented, affecting the flow of thought and productivity. Add to this the collaborative nature of design and the need to work with other designers and external agencies, and the potential for delay in reaching agreement and/or achieving the necessary statutory consents and permits is considerable. Significant delays are likely between different phases in the design process, thus there is always a danger that the synergy between conceptual designs and detailed designs, and between detailed designs and construction, can be affected adversely. Add in some latitude for designers' overwhelming and paralysing periods of indecision as they seek to find the best solution for a poorly defined problem, and the potential for chaos is high. That is why the whole design and construction process needs very careful consideration and planning – the process must be controlled, both at the individual project level and within the diverse organisations that are contributing different aspects to the project. Important considerations are the management of information, knowledge, people and resources (such as IT) that will facilitate efficient communications and co-ordination.

The detailer's milieu

It is easy to get carried away with the act of detailing. Too much attention to a small area can result in selective vision with the danger of ignoring the more obvious and important issues. Chess players are familiar with this phenomenon (known as 'chess blindness') where the most obvious move is overlooked, with dire consequences. Overall responsibility for design quality will lie with the design manager (ultimate responsibility lies with the organisation's directors or partners); however, individuals must take responsibility for their actions and consequent decisions. A degree of self-management is an important requirement in order to maintain progress of the programme. Too much time can easily disappear as the detailer struggles with seemingly insurmountable detailing issues, with the result that the remaining design is rushed and the probability of mistakes occurring is increased. We must remember that detail drawings and written specifications are produced with the sole aim of communicating the designer's abstract thoughts to the mind of the contractor, who will endeavour to implement such instructions in the form of a physical artefact. Instructions must be clear, unambiguous and free of errors.

In the design office, the environment in which details are drawn and specifications written, there needs to be a constant evaluation of design work and the process by which it comes about (see Fig. C4.2). For this we need a very valuable resource, time, for the following activities:

Fig. C4.2 The detailer's milieu. A busy designer (using new and less-new technologies and information).

- to research, i.e. look at what others have done, collect and assimilate information;
- to monitor manufacturers' information about new products;
- to develop the detail, be it from first principles or adapted from standard solutions;
- to check the detail (for compliance with relevant regulations, client requirements, and for errors);
- to issue the detail to those who need the information;
- to monitor the detail in practice (feedback). Was it easy to build? Has the assembly performed as required?

This information is vital for the development of the detailer's personal knowledge and the collective organisational knowledge of the office, from which other detailers may draw inspiration.

Detailing is not an activity that should be done in isolation. We need information and knowledge from those more familiar with particular materials and products than we can be, namely, the manufacturers, suppliers and trades-people. Relationships with individuals and organisations need to be forged and nurtured to enable communication and co-operation towards a common goal (see Chapter C5).

Design control in the office

A variety of managerial tools may be employed in an attempt to control the quality of design activity and hence give some degree of consistency to the designs produced by a particular office. There are various schools of thought as to which may be most appropriate; however, the most important criterion is that the management system must work for the design office and its members, giving them a framework in which to produce creative and consistent designs. It is also important that the process is not segmented into 'manageable packages' without providing the necessary effort to integrate the work packages, otherwise there is a danger that the boundaries between the packages of work can act as a barrier to communication and creative thought transfer. Whatever method of management adopted by individual design offices it is important that the design manager can support the people he or she represents and has the strength to see through ideas from inception to completion. In addition to quality management systems there are three complementary methods of controlling design – design reviews, checking mechanisms and internal critiques. To a certain extent all are concerned with co-ordination of information from a variety of sources, communication between interested parties and the creation and maintenance of an effective decision-making culture, thus allowing the project to progress within the time frame and budget. More specifically:

- design reviews (in line with ISO 9000 series/quality management);
- internal design critiques;
- checking (by design manager). This may be linked to design reviews and critiques, but is a separate function. All information must be 'signed off' before it leaves the office;
- programming to enhance and encourage conceptual detailing – by this we mean allowing adequate time to explore alternative solutions.

The end result is information, and this also has to be co-ordinated and managed. Clearly there is a need to control the input from other consultants, specialist suppliers and manufacturers (usually located in different offices to the detailer) and hence control the flow of information at organisational and project levels. Co-ordination of resources and information remains a challenge, especially when different detailers are working in different locations and for different organisations, although this is greatly assisted through sophisticated IT software. Design managers need to develop a culture which encourages 'ownership' (regardless of the particular design management style employed in the office). This is mainly achieved through interpersonal communication and motivation, while working within a managerial framework.

Design and engineering organisations, like any other business enterprise, need to make a profit on their turnover. The detail design phase is one of the most demanding in terms of the skills and time required, thus the tendency for costs and time to overrun if adequate managerial control is not exerted is ever present. Programming and resourcing are important concerns. Offices usually contain professionals with different skills and varying levels of experience. Inexperienced staff require adequate supervision during the detailing phase, while very experienced staff need some encouragement to move away from their tried and tested methods of detailing – they need to innovate – if we are to move towards buildings that are detailed in a more sustainable manner. It is at this juncture that we need to consider the issue of design liability. Innovative details increase the organisation's exposure to risk and so time is needed to research the detail and possibly test the detail thoroughly before implementation, a philosophy exploited to its fullest potential by, for example, Renzo Piano with his 'workshop' approach.

Design control during construction

It is important to be in a position to control details during the construction phase; however, the type of contractual arrangement chosen earlier in the process will have determined who has responsibility for decisions made during construction. In collaborative working arrangements based on the expertise of technology clusters this may not necessarily be a problem;

Fig. C4.3   Information being transformed into a completed building.

however, in more traditional working arrangements the issue of who controls the decision-making (designer or contractor) may have a significant bearing on the overall quality of the finished building (see Fig. C4.3).

It is rare to work on projects where details are not altered after they have been agreed and issued. Reasons for alteration may be quite varied, but are usually down to the following factors:

- to aid constructability;
- delivery/supply problems;
- time pressures;
- cost pressures.

Changing details and substituting products may be undertaken with or without the designer's knowledge. With the designer's consent is obviously the preferred option.

The thinking organisation

Individuals work within, and therefore contribute to, the prevailing culture of their particular design office, that is, they work within the organisational boundaries of a particular business. This organisational culture is likely to be disposed towards an attitude of openness and change at one end of the spectrum or a closed culture unwilling (or unable) to change at the other. This culture will influence the organisation's attitude to architectural design and with it the likelihood of adoption or rejection of new ideas, methods and products. At one extreme are the design offices where the culture is not to challenge or change established methods of dealing with design problems. In such offices standard details and specifications are used extensively and new information is sought only when situations force such action, hence the status quo will prevail, change will be very gradual and the use of innovative details is unlikely. At the opposite end of the scale are the design offices that are orientated towards change and the embrace of new ideas and knowledge. In these offices standard details and specifications are used sparingly, with the office seeking to innovate with each new project. These innovative design offices, working in collaboration with equally innovative manufacturers, suppliers and contractors, demonstrate new ideas and hence set a fashion for the majority to follow. The majority of design offices are positioned somewhere between these two extremes, their position shifting as they seek to satisfy the requirements of different clients.

Against the backdrop of an ever-competitive construction sector, with its focus on change, is our search for knowledge. Creative organisations survive on their capacity for learning and building knowledge, the better they are able to incorporate and utilise knowledge, the better they are at integrating, synthesising, sharing, incorporating and adapting, and hence the greater their likelihood of success. Although definitions of knowledge vary between organisations, one factor common to all is that knowledge is always changing, that is, it has a limited shelf life. So the capacity to refresh and renew knowledge is the key to competitive advantage. This is a collective task in which members of the office create and share knowledge through group and team working, continually reflecting on the value of the knowledge before them and on the associated learning process. It is the process of organisational knowledge creation and its transfer that needs to be recognised and hence managed. This is best done within a 'learning' or 'thinking' organisation

Fig. C4.4   The thinking organisation. A team should be and is more than one or other of its members. The whole is even more than the sum of its parts or participants. A new genius (can) come(s) from a team.

(see Fig. C4.4) in which the focus of activities is knowledge-based rather than task-based.

Good design offices encourage and foster a reflective attitude to all aspects of the design process and will try to programme work to allow individuals time for some degree of reflection, essentially time to 'think'. Because the benefits gained from reflection outweigh the additional time programmed, this does not necessarily add cost to the project. Mistakes tend to be fewer and the quality of thought will manifest itself in the ensuing designs and details. Thinking organisations can support their drive for excellence through considered use of continuing professional development (CPD) and training programmes. Empowering employees and encouraging them to develop and share their knowledge with other organisation members is an underlying factor in the development of best practice. Best practice is about adding to the intellectual capital of the organisation (and in turn, society). To engage in best practice we need a constant source of accurate and accessible information and knowledge. We must be open to new information from outside the organisation. This information has to be analysed, filtered (rejected, used and/or stored for future reference) and built upon to the benefit of the design organisation and its individual projects. Thus information management and the application of knowledge are key to the running of a design organisation. It follows that organisational knowledge must be constantly re-freshed, through:

- encouraging all office members to engage in reflective prac-tice;
- all members undertaking relevant continuing professional development;
- collaborating with universities on research projects;
- engaging in work-based research;
- encouraging new staff (especially recent graduates) to con-tribute their ideas.

Developing creative clusters

With specific reference to joint solutions, we can encourage a creative approach through the development of creative tech-nology clusters to specifically challenge and fundamentally rethink the way we approach details and detailing. This was touched upon in Chapter A2 and is revisited here because it is an issue for how individual projects are resourced and the extent to which offices engage in research and development. The philosophy behind the creation of creative clusters is to integrate design and production knowledge for the mu-tual benefit of all concerned with the project. These clusters should also endeavour to think differently with the intention of bettering our current approach to detailing. From a man-agement perspective our overwhelming concern is with the amount of time available. To set up creative clusters specifi-cally to address joint solutions requires time that someone, somehow, has to pay for. This brings us on to the economics of projects.

Professional fees may be charged as a percentage rate of the overall construction cost or as a fixed fee (which in practice is usually calculated on an estimated construction cost). The prob-lem with percentage fees as seen from the client's perspective is that there appears to be no incentive to reduce construction costs, although most professionals would disagree with this view (the primary argument being that they are profession-als and therefore they act with integrity, and also that getting the cost down may lead to further commissions). A fixed fee may provide for more opportunity to develop details from first principles; however, the fee must be agreed at the correct level. With considerable pressure to reduce professional fees, and hence the amount of time devoted to design and production, the possibility of having adequate time to engage in research and development activity for individual projects for the majority of projects is unlikely. There is a paradox here. Cutting time in the early stages of design may prove to be expensive further along the chain; changes early in the supply chain can have the greatest impact on the efficiency of the project. We would argue for more time here and with it a fundamental rethink about how projects are financed and managed. This is clearly demonstrated in the 'iceberg' theory (see Fig. C4.5) of hidden costs. Eco-tax is a small step towards resolving the problem, although now may be the time for a fundamental rethink about

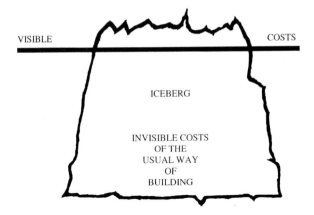

VISIBLE   COSTS

ICEBERG

INVISIBLE COSTS
OF THE
USUAL WAY
OF
BUILDING

SOLUTION:
HEALTHY AND ENVIRONMENTAL-CONSCIOUS
BUILDING
FOR A
SUSTAINABLE DEVELOPMENT

Fig. C4.5 The 'iceberg' theory shows that the invisible costs of our usual method of producing buildings (and many other modern goods) are approximately ten times higher than the costs paid by the client directly. The hidden costs of present and future expenses for the reparation of environmental damage and pollution as well as health hazards (sometimes even without success) – and the difference between justifiable and criminally low rates for labour and resources in the Third World – are in total certainly more than ten times higher than what we are used to paying. Sustainable building actually means having none or hardly any of those invisible costs.

how we approach and manage our projects with an emphasis on whole-life performance. This must be seen as an investment for our future. We need to formulate the time and hence the revenue required to develop a knowledge-based approach rather than a process one, as a mechanism to promote long-term thinking. This is an area that needs further debate and development within the whole-life philosophy; all actors need to be engaged and responsible.

Practical considerations

In the spirit of collaboration and the pursuit of knowledge there are a number of practical considerations that may help in the pursuit of more environmentally friendly joint solutions (Figs C4.6 and C4.7). They are addressed here from a number of different perspectives.

The office

Design managers need to set clear and realistic objectives for their staff. They should:

- discuss ecological issues and human factors with clients at the briefing stage (and be prepared to educate and inform as necessary);
- provide sensitive programming (to allow adequate time to explore alternatives);
- provide adequate information about alternative, more ecological, solutions;
- try to work with contractors (and consultants) who are sympathetic to green issues and who have their own policies and checklists in place;
- ensure feedback mechanisms are in place and are adhered to;
- provide clear guidance to office members about risk and associated issues that colour decision-making.

Fig. C4.6

Fig. C4.7

Individual designers and engineers

Detailers need to:

- constantly re-evaluate the details being used;
- monitor their own progress against set programmed targets;
- think about the building users and provide them with the necessary tools and information to help them run the building economically and ecologically;
- use feedback to enhance the individual knowledge base;
- work within an ethical framework.

Constructors

Those charged with assembling the building are also able to assist in the drive for sustainable construction by:

- working closely with the detailers to provide feedback and suggestions about constructability to reduce wastage on site;
- resisting pressure to substitute specified products and resisting the temptation to adjust agreed details unless absolutely necessary;
- trying to ensure the joint is assembled as detailed and specified, thus helping to ensure the joint performs as intended;
- working towards collaboration, using technology clusters to maximise knowledge transfer and feedback.

Manufacturers

Manufacturers and material suppliers can help designers in their decision-making by:

- supplying accurate information about the ecological credentials of products;
- working with designers and constructors to improve the reuse and recycling of products at the end of their service life;
- working towards the continual improvement of products through incremental innovation;

- introducing new, innovative products and systems to suit a more responsible approach to construction;
- collaborating with other manufacturers and suppliers with a view to addressing joint-specific, rather than product-specific, solutions.

Clients

As sponsors of individual projects, clients must recognise their responsibilities and should:

- take responsibility for their choices, that is, embrace whole-life costing and environmental ideals;
- adopt an ethical approach;
- commission professionals who are committed to higher values, that is, ensure their competences are compatible.

Users

All participants in the design and construction process must do more to include the views and requirements of the building users. However, users have a responsibility to be proactive on this matter and should:

- try to ensure that their experiences are fed back to design professionals, without waiting to be asked;
- engage in post-occupancy evaluation methods with a view to constantly improving our knowledge base.

C5 COLLABORATIVE WORKING

Technology is characterised by a high degree of complexity. In practice this demands the co-operation and collaboration of a variety of actors. Not only scientists, designers and technologists, but also specialists in the fields of finance, economics, politics, social sciences and management (to name but a few), need to be brought together to solve technological problems. Moreover we must not forget that various governmental departments, and particularly our clients, are co-shaping the technological processes (and hence the results) through their legislative frameworks and their particular space/building requirements respectively. Too often we experience a lack of real integration and co-operation, leading to duplicated work and missed opportunities. In a time of growing environmental consciousness, which is also created by the manner in which technology is developed and applied, we have to consider a (more) harmonious collaboration.

Co-operation and communication

All human working processes and all results within our culture are to a lesser or greater extent based on co-operation and communication. Even the existence of a hermit depends on the fact that other individuals in society work together. Sometimes it may be that co-operation and consensus instinctively take place, like in the case of 'simple things' and within so-called primitive cultures. However, in our busy and highly interconnected world with many complicated relationships and pressure to perform, nothing is less natural than automatic co-operation and consensus: this includes design, planning and building activities.

In his video presentation *The Global Brain* Peter Russell demonstrated the necessity of working together on various levels if we want to survive as humankind. In the context of design, and participation in design, it is necessary to apply efficient methods and techniques to reach the aims of a harmonious working process and integrated results (Fig. C5.1). This means that we need to collaborate and communicate effectively at all stages with the life cycle of a building. In the context of developing collaborative working arrangements we need to recognise that communication occurs on four different levels. These are:

- Intrapersonal communication enables an individual to process information; only one person is involved, that is, it is concerned with the thought process.
- Interpersonal communication enables individuals to establish and maintain relationships, and is concerned with the exchange of information between two people.
- Small-group communication enables members of work groups to co-ordinate activities, and involves three or more people (see Fig. C5.3; five to six people is a maximum if the group is to be effective).
- Multi-group communication enables different work groups to co-ordinate their efforts. This is an important consideration in the context of a construction project.

In addition to the different levels of communication, we all tend to use slightly different language to express our wants and feelings, and so it is important to make some effort to make sure

Fig. C5.1   Collaborative work by MHP (method of holistic participation). The MHP logo shows a woven or rather a weaving structure of various, necessary lines of development, influencing and integrating with each other in a role-rotating consulting process, towards consensus and optimisation.

that the sender and receivers of the message understand one another if misunderstanding and errors are to be avoided.

Teamwork method

Konrad Wachsmann (Fig. C5.2) and Walter Gropius introduced a teamwork method for the development of complex building concepts in the 1940s. Although they never mentioned the possible source(s) of their system, the essence of their method can be found in Native American and Indonesian culture where problems were solved in a 'democratic' and harmonious way

Fig. C5.2   Konrad Wachsmann. Together with Walter Gropius he introduced the principle of teamwork into building. The method of role-changing consultation towards problem-solving was already known and practised by many indigenous people in different parts of the world.

Fig. C5.3   A team approach (the authors working on this book).

within the tribe. Integral, holistic functioning is a natural principle in the processes of nature and in nature as a dynamic wholeness. Dynamic balance is a result of holistic and repeatedly integrated processes. From medieval times we know about the mystic seven synchronities (*die sieben Gleichzeitigkeiten*). It was said that a human being is able – at the peak of his or her powers – to see or remember seven items at the same time in order to combine them creatively to produce a new discovery or artefact, like a piece of art, a scientific technological invention or an architectural design. So, an individual can exercise this synchronising method or technique systematically to reach balanced results on his or her own, that is, engage in intrapersonal communication.

Today everyone is influenced by and also dependent on many factors due to the rise of specialisms and the related division and fragmentation of working processes. This interconnectivity of many participants places additional pressures on the ability to communicate and share information and knowledge. This is especially true of the design process, which was formerly very individual and hence more personal than it is today. Now everyone is dependent in some way on other players in order to complete tasks and realise goals. Thus interpersonal communication, intra-organisational and inter-organisational communication are particularly pertinent (in a world of mass communication).

In building techniques and science a horizontal (democratic) structure of the various components responsible for the final artefact was introduced and can be seen as a turning point like the title of Wachsmann's (1959) publication, *Wendepunkt im Bauen*. In the 1950s there was very little awareness of the ecological aspects, the specific human factors and environmental problems. Therefore these new factors had to be added to this first total view of building components, which was formulated by Konrad Wachsmann and supported by Walter Gropius. Finally these additions led to the holistic metamodel of an integral biological architecture.

Holistic participation method

The method of holistic participation (MHP; see Fig. C5.1) was developed by Peter Schmid following his training with Konrad Wachsmann during international academic summer courses in

Salzburg, Austria, from 1956 to 1960. After this development the teamwork method was applied numerous times with various subjects and groups of different capability and size in several countries. The MHP method was presented at the International Design Participation conference held at Eindhoven University of Technology in April 1985, as a way to collaborate and participate together in a common design for a better future. In some respects the method is based on the old village model, where people live together in harmony; here the community is concerned with developing an ecologically responsible and healthy environment through the use of bio-logical architecture. In the education programmes of Eindhoven University of Technology the method is used for 'teamwork and integration' exercises, including groups of students from other institutions worldwide. Indeed, the method has found a place in other fields, such as education, physics and even politics, where politicians have used the workshops to confront ecological issues, such as environmental pollution. So we see a growing number of interested participants gaining from this method.

Definitions

Before we proceed further it is necessary to give some definitions. 'Holism' is a theory of wholeness, *Ganzheit*, totality, originating in Greece. 'Holistic' describes a balanced and integrated complexity. 'Participating', from Latin *pars*, a part, means to be and to act as a part of a larger order or higher totality or wholeness.

In the context of holistic participation, other important terms are:

- co-operation: working together generally;
- teamwork: specially structured co-operation;
- co-ordination: multidisciplinary, interdisciplinary organisation (synthesise);
- integration: composition, *Gestaltung* or co-ordination;
- consensus: common (parallel) sense and complementary addition to each other;
- method: clear, systematic and efficient way of problem-solving;
- process: the path, the way (including causes and conditions);
- result: the aim, the answer, the solution, the goal, the outcome of all participating influences.

Aims

According to Zen and some other philosophies dealing with self-realisation, the path and the goal are one, which is useful for all participants of a team or a working group. The aims are:

- to co-operate in a convenient way, to be able to handle conflicts, to work together in a stimulating, enjoyable and efficient manner; and
- to reach satisfying solutions that not only fit the tasks, problems and questions posed (see Fig. C5.4) but also satisfy the needs and intentions of the participants and/or clients.

The general starting point for holistic participation is the fact that, in order to survive, there are innumerable tasks we have to fulfil in our social life together in large and small groups or teams (see Fig. C5.5). Design in the framework of shaping our built environment belongs or leads to the conditions responsi-

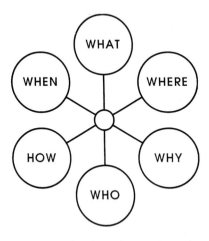

Fig. C5.4   The six topic questions. A good question is already half an answer. Whatever the problem might be – e.g. detailing and conceptualisation – the topic questions answered or solved bring us to the result.

DECIDE TO NETWORK

USE EVERY LETTER YOU WRITE
EVERY CONVERSATION YOU HAVE
EVERY MEETING YOU ATTEND
TO EXPRESS YOUR FUNDAMENTAL BELIEFS AND DREAMS
AFFIRM TO OTHERS THE VISION OF THE WORLD YOU WANT
NETWORK THROUGH THOUGHT
NETWORK THROUGH ACTION
NETWORK THROUGH LOVE
NETWORK THROUGH THE SPIRIT
YOU ARE THE CENTRE OF A NETWORK
YOU ARE THE CENTRE OF THE WORLD
YOU ARE A FREE, IMMENSELY POWERFUL SOURCE OF LIFE
AND GOODNESS
AFFIRM IT
SPREAD IT
RADIATE IT
THINK DAY AND NIGHT ABOUT IT
AND YOU WILL SEE A MIRACLE HAPPEN:
THE GREATNESS OF YOUR OWN LIFE
IN A WORLD OF BIG POWERS, MEDIA, AND MONOPOLIES
BUT OF FIVE BILLION INDIVIDUALS
NETWORKING IS THE NEW FREEDOM
THE NEW DEMOCRACY
A NEW FORM OF HAPPINESS

ROBERT MULLER

Fig. C5.5 Decide to network. Robert Muller, former Assistant Secretary-General of the United Nations, is the author of this summons. Teamwork, holistic participation extended to a global scale, as it is needed for sustainable development in a smaller world. (Copyright held by Peter Schmid.)

ble for our more or less common existence. So, the aims of the holistic participation method are:

- to include, at least in principle, and/or in a representative way, all relevant aspects or factors and all concerned participants;
- to gain basic qualities of human and ecological conditions or in other words an integral bio-logical approach, carried by the main characteristics of *bios* and *logos*, leading to healthy and satisfying results.

Planning support systems are always closely related to the co-operation of more than one person or group of people. Hence teamwork and groupwork are an important part in order to support (design) decisions or systematic and methodical collaboration and co-operation or participation. A systematic, practical and organised approach is required to realise these participatory processes, and a method is described below.

Holistic participation: the method

In the context of the argument presented in this book it is beneficial to work from a more abstract and general approach to a more concrete and specific one. Continuation of the work done by others, additional work, the use of 'mental stealing' and the 'creativity of conflict' hold an important place here. The assembly of the team will vary depending on the task being addressed, but we would strongly urge the inclusion of the client or a client's representative to contribute to and hence own the resultant decisions. The principle of holistic participation works as a relatively straightforward method.

(1) The (main) task or problem, which in the case of design is always a complex one, has to be divided into the various partial problems, aspects or factors. This is done according to the wishes and ideas of the participants.

(2) The whole team has to be divided into small working groups (mini-teams) with ideally three members in each group. Each group should deal with an individual factor, so the number of groups should correspond to the number of factors identified earlier.

(3) After these processes of division, discussed with the whole team, each small working group goes on to investigate one of the partial problems or factors independently from the other groups.

(4) After this investigation period is complete, all the members come together again as a larger group to inform each other of the outcome of their work. Each group will choose an individual to present their ideas and then when each group has 'spoken' other members of the groups are invited to speak, thus allowing an open and representative discussion.

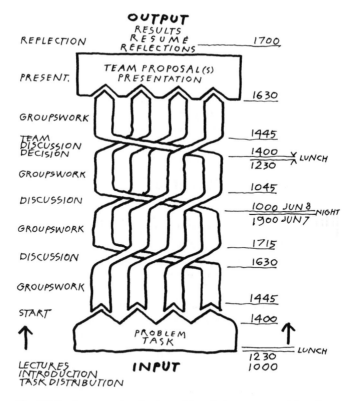

OUTPUT

REFLECTION — RESULTS / RESUME / REFLECTIONS — 1700

PRESENT. — TEAM PROPOSAL(S) / PRESENTATION — 1630

GROUPSWORK — 1445

TEAM DISCUSSION DECISION — 1400 / LUNCH / 1230

GROUPSWORK — 1045

DISCUSSION — 1000 JUN 8 / NIGHT / 1900 JUN 7

GROUPSWORK — 1715

DISCUSSION — 1630

GROUPSWORK — 1445

START — 1400

PROBLEM TASK

INPUT — 1230 / LUNCH / 1000

LECTURES / INTRODUCTION / TASK DISTRIBUTION

Fig. C5.6   An example of a timetable split into, or containing, four groups (or individuals) with their own (changing) subjects – the four main aspects or components of the problem (function, structure, material, process) and its solution.

(5) After this information sharing, discussion and consultation period, all working groups change the subject and continue to investigate according to this pattern.

(6) This 'game' will continue as long as necessary to give everyone the chance to investigate each of the partial problems or factors. At that point in the cycle the 'rotating' and 'weaving' experience is finished.

(7) It is always practical to group the participants, to structure the partial problems or factors and the time in such a way that the integration process can be organised and managed (see Figs C5.6 and C5.7).

(8) This 'rotating' or 'weaving' process can be continued for a second (or third or fourth) time in making a design ready for realisation. By moving from the abstract towards the specific through well-structured and functional group work it has been proven that design development can be

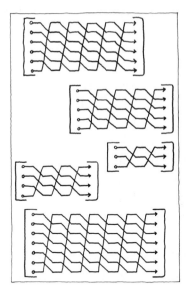

Fig. C5.7   More examples of timetables or better working schemes. The varieties show the flexibility of the method as to the number of the participants, the number of the aspects or components and the available time.

achieved quickly and effectively. All participants have a sense of ownership of the results.

(9) Consultants and experts from outside the team should participate in the discussions as early as possible. Of course it is advisable to use all kind of available audio-visual methods, models and clear text, sketches, drawings, and so on, for deeper research as well as better information and presentation.

(10) In ideal circumstances and with a well-trained team the group work process is extremely enjoyable and the results will emerge in a fun and creative way without too much effort.

(11) Alongside the 'serious' applications of the method it may be useful to include some socio-psychological and creativity games.

Future developments

Collaboration and co-operation are needed more than ever before. The integration of design and construction processes is an obvious and pressing consideration for clients, participants and building users alike, and an area in which holistic participation methods can bring these cultures together and hence help to realise value for all. On a related but wider agenda there are two main problems that can be addressed and action facilitated by using the method – first, facing up to the environmental impact of construction activities and building usage in response to our global ecological crisis, and second, the necessity for different (power) groups to come together in order to reach some consensus for our common survival.

After looking back to the medieval idea of a creative process, the experience of the Wachsmann seminars and the very recent participation workshops, we can look forward to the future of design participation and planning support systems. It is a matter of fact that only a conscious and harmonious participation leads to good co-operation, and only through good co-operation will we survive. Multiple learning processes bring us to a higher level and quality of existence and make us more conscious of our common basic needs and aims.

One of the main conditions to attain these qualities is probably methodical co-operation. In fact the method could be applied to every thinkable (complex) task in the field of planning and building design including a focus on detail, as well as in all other disciplines. We can imagine that, as in an orchestra, various teams on various subjects, working together, will design and build a harmonious environment that fits – in a democratic way – the needs of all participants and all concerned and committed people.

A design for a 'house for another future', a prototype and pilot project fully based on a health and environment scenario (SBS-free and environmentally conscious), has already been worked out by means of the MHP.

The starting point for a holistic design participation process in architecture, building and planning is based on methodical, enjoyable and stimulating co-operation in order to finally reach efficient and optimised results. The necessary consensus of the participants may be fed by the creativity of conflict, but all important aspects, components and factors have to influence, as relevant causes, the final effects. Mankind has always had to handle diverse, sometimes complicated, ingredients to shape a complex totality on various levels. Synchronicity, simultaneity, balance and equilibrium were always aims in the design process. Wachsmann was the first to introduce a teamwork method that fitted these demands (*Forderungen*); by means of systematic working and thorough discussion, research can be conducted and information exchanged. Considerable training of this kind has already been developed and has taken place in many countries (see Figs C5.8, C5.9 and C5.10). Hence, there is already enough positive and promising experience from the past and very recent past for further applications in the future. The method can be expanded to several other fields. Hopefully the method of holistic participation can make a practical contribution to our planned and built environment, extending beyond detailing to include a higher general responsibility to

Fig. C5.8 Some examples of the outcome from the work of teams. Workshop results in different countries from the last decades. Attention to detail as well as the whole is possible. By means of MHP it is even easy and enjoyable.

humankind and the environment. We believe that future genius in art, science and technology will be born in the harmonious co-operation of the team.

Fig. C5.9 Tools should always serve to enhance the quality of life through the quality of building and its details.

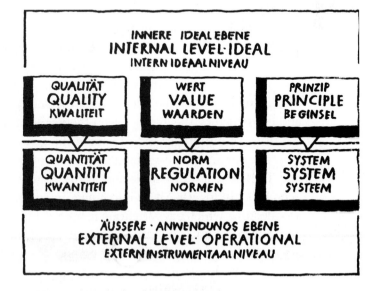

Fig. C5.10 Values should always guide regulations. Quality of values and principles should always come before regulations and systems.

Afterword

Given the scope of this book, a conclusion would be inappropriate; instead we offer a few final words by way of an afterword.

As champions of the products that we specify, the decisions we take will have a small but collectively significant effect on our built environment, our wellbeing and our natural environment. Developing a desire and also the intention to think and act differently should be inherent in the education and training of built environment professionals, regardless of their particular role or job function. The intention of this book has been to try to stimulate such thinking by way of some theory, some practical tools, and ideas that can be explored and refined in education and carried through into the workplace where decisions entail consequences. Principles of architectural detailing have been discussed and explained with that in mind. We have covered the need for responsible detailing and conveyed, we hope, the fascination of the task. While there is a long tradition of detailing in vernacular architecture, there is a much shorter tradition in developing details from the desk. The gap between the workshop, the site and the (virtual) desk is perhaps obvious and needs to be tackled.

The challenge is continuous. The need is imperative to engage in effective communication, produce timely and accurate information, use our knowledge and develop the necessary competences to act in a more ethical manner. A further issue is the division between the intentions of the designers, producers and constructors, the gap between the needs of the client and the users of buildings, and of course the growing separation between our artificially created environments and our natural one. These current and, some may argue, urgent problems have been brought together here into a new integrated approach to architecture, which pays attention to both detailing and human and ecological quality of life. Associated with this philosophy are a number of tools for developing and designing, researching and educating, aimed at fostering a proper, harmonious, dynamically balanced built environment, with physical details at its nucleus.

Now encouraged to think differently, it is up to the readers of this book to adopt these principles and to place a new value on the detail of our decisions and actions. It would be a mistake to assume that everything has already been done: we are just at the start.

Appendices

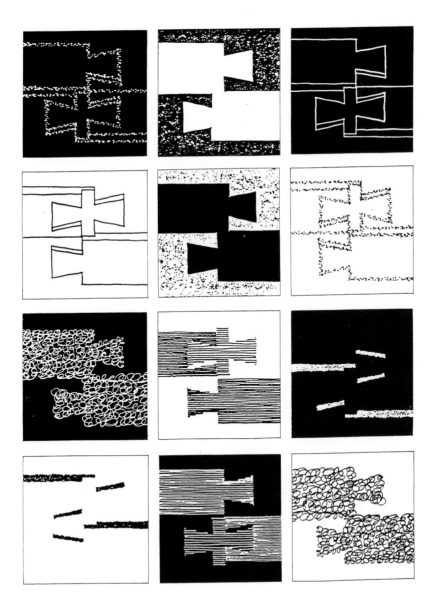

1 RECOMMENDED READING

Recommending further reading is not an easy task, especially in a book of this kind. We are aware that different individuals have differing requirements and tastes and so what we find educational and inspiring may not suit everyone. However, it is useful to put down a few markers for readers to follow should they so wish.

Communication

Blyth, A. & Worthington, J. (2001) *Managing the Brief for Better Design.* Spon Press, London.

Emmitt, S. & Gorse, C. (2003) *Construction Communication.* Blackwell Publishing, Oxford.

Detailing and design data

Emmitt, S. (2002) *Architectural Technology.* Blackwell Publishing, Oxford.

Groak, S. (1992) *The Idea of Building: thought and action in the design and production of buildings.* E & FN Spon, London.

Neufert, E. & Neufert, P. (2002) *Architects' Data*, 3rd edn. Blackwell Publishing, Oxford.

Olie, J.C.M. (1996) *A Typology of Joints: supporting sustainable development in building.* PhD thesis, Bouwstenen 42, Eindhoven University of Technology, Eindhoven.

Wachsmann, K. (1959) *Wendepunkt im Bauen.* Published in English (1961) *The Turning Point of Building: structure and design.* Reinhold Publishing Corporation, New York.

Environmental issues

Erkelens, P.A., de Jonge, S. & van Vliet, A.A.M (eds) (2002) *Beyond Sustainable Building: balancing between best-practice and utopian concepts*. Bouwstenen 65, Eindhoven University of Technology, Eindhoven.

Schmid, P. (2000) *The Art, Science, Technology and Wisdom to Build*, Eindhoven University of Technology, Eindhoven.

Van der Ryn, S. & McCowan, S. (1995) *Ecological Design*. Island Press, Washington DC.

Specification

Anderson, J., Shiers, D & Sinclair, M. (2002) *Green Guide to Specification*. Blackwell Publishing, Oxford.

Emmitt, S. & Yeomans, D.T. (2001) *Specifying Buildings: a design management approach*. Butterworth-Heinemann, Oxford.

References

Chapter A3

Agenda 21: World Commission on Environment and Development (1987) *Our Common Future* (The Brundlandt Report). Oxford University Press, Oxford.

Chapter A4

Halliday, S. (2000) *Green Guide to the Architect's Job Book*. RIBA Publications, London.

Chapter C2

Alexander, C. (1964) *Notes on the Synthesis of Form*. Harvard University Press, Cambridge, MA.

Chapter C5

Russell, P. (1983) *The Global Brain* (video presentation; directed by Chris Hall). Putman Publishing Group. See also Russell, P. (1983) *The Global Brain*. Putman Publishing Group.

2 GUIDANCE FOR STUDENTS

The manner in which students are taught varies between institutions and within subject areas. We are conscious of the fact that many students of their subject appreciate additional tasks that they can pursue in their own time. With this in mind we have prepared a few tasks that anyone, regardless of age or ability, can attempt. Each task includes self-reflection, i.e. what have you discovered through undertaking the task?

Essential to learning and individual development is the ability to learn from the work of others. This was discussed in Chapter A3, but it may be worth re-emphasising the need for self-motivation and the desire to constantly look and challenge what we see through the tools listed below. It is vital to record the date, the location, any references, etc. on every piece of work for future referral.

- The sketchbook (a size that is easy to carry around, A5 or A4) for sketching and taking notes. A laptop computer may serve a similar function.
- Measured drawings (then analyse, think about what's behind the façade).
- Photographic records, still and video clips.
- Examples of others' work, from journals, etc.
- Manufacturers' information. Analyse literature critically. Do not take everything at face value, do some research and check the claims presented in the literature.

A few simple student exercises that may be used as the basis of tutorial discussions, and can equally be undertaken individually or by groups, are offered here. The intention is to make us think and act a little differently.

Exercise 1: Performance requirements

Consider the implications of a simple change in the performance requirements for, say, the insulation value (U value) of the
external wall of a house. For this exercise our wall is 8 metres
long and 2.4 metres high. The wall has one door with opening size 1 m × 2.2 m and two windows each with opening size
2 m × 1.5 m. Detailing this wall with its windows and door is
a relatively straightforward activity if we comply with current
building codes. We can be lazy and apply standard solutions
or we can approach the problem using the advice given in this
book.

Now, make things a little more difficult and interesting. Double the thermal performance required under the current building codes, for example, if the U value is 0.2, make it 0.1. What is
the implication for your details? It is unlikely that 'standard'
solutions can be found.

Now double the performance requirements again (staying
with the example above, this would make the U value 0.05).
Now tackle the detailing of the wall.

Q: Reflecting on your actions, what have you learned?

Exercise 2: Disassembly as a primary requirement

Take your current, or a previous, design project, and change the
primary requirement of the brief. The primary requirement is
to disassemble the building at a set time in the future, say five
years, without producing any waste. How do you detail your
building to achieve this? What are the design life and service
life of individual components? Can you achieve the task by
using standard components?

Q: Reflecting on your actions, what have you learned?

Exercise 3: A new building system

Develop a new building based primarily on the use of one material, for example, wood, plant material, clay, etc. The building should fit within a $7 \times 7 \times 7$ m cube.

All human-ecological qualities should be fully respected in order to enrich the experience and health of those using the building. Soft and passive building technologies should be used to create and maintain a comfortable indoor climate throughout the year.

The building should be drawn in 3D and with all horizontal and vertical sections to illustrate all of the main joints and intersections. All joint solutions should be presented at a scale of $1:5$, or even $1:1$. A digital or physical model may help in developing the design solution and in communicating the intention. The design proposal should be accompanied by a short written description that outlines and helps to justify the approach taken.

Q: Reflecting on your actions, what have you learned?

Exercise 4: Developing new details

Take a typical detail, for example a window-frame joint, and use the nine-plus-one step procedure to create a new detail, following the method described in Chapter C3.

This exercise can be carried out by an individual or by a group of students (using MHP) by taking a building and looking at the main details. The building could be one that is used by students or it could be a well-known building featured in books and journals.

These exercises can be carried out quickly and discussed in a tutorial, or they can form the basis for further development.

Q: Reflecting on your actions, what have you learned?

INDEX